Fundamentals of Information Risk Management Auditing

An Introduction for Managers and Auditors

Fundamentals of Information Risk Management Auditing

An Introduction for Managers and Auditors

Christopher Wright

itgp™

IT Governance Publishing

Every possible effort has been made to ensure that the information contained in this book is accurate at the time of going to press, and the publisher and the author cannot accept responsibility for any errors or omissions, however caused. Any opinions expressed in this book are those of the author, not the publisher. Websites identified are for reference only, not endorsement, and any website visits are at the reader's own risk. No responsibility for loss or damage occasioned to any person acting, or refraining from action, as a result of the material in this publication can be accepted by the publisher or the author.

Apart from any fair dealing for the purposes of research or private study, or criticism or review, as permitted under the Copyright, Designs and Patents Act 1988, this publication may only be reproduced, stored or transmitted, in any form, or by any means, with the prior permission in writing of the publisher or, in the case of reprographic reproduction, in accordance with the terms of licences issued by the Copyright Licensing Agency. Enquiries concerning reproduction outside those terms should be sent to the publisher at the following address:

IT Governance Publishing
IT Governance Limited
Unit 3, Clive Court
Bartholomew's Walk
Cambridgeshire Business Park
Ely
Cambridgeshire
CB7 4EA
United Kingdom
www.itgovernance.co.uk

The author has asserted the rights of the author under the Copyright, Designs and Patents Act, 1988, to be identified as the author of this work.

First published in the United Kingdom in 2016
by IT Governance Publishing.

ISBN 978-1-84928-815-6

FOREWORD

It's often said that we live in the 'Information Age'. When we consider our lives and how important information has become over the last 20 or so years, it is amazing. Every decision we make is based on information – be it our choice of holiday, career, new car, or where to live. Thanks to social networking, we know more about what our friends, family and associates are doing right now (often more than we would like to know!). Events on the far side of the world are streamed to us in real time. We can search for answers to the most obscure questions imaginable – even during the quiz at our local pubs. We can watch movies, read books from a library of many works, check out our contacts, and review the news and share prices – all from our telephones and mobile devices – almost anywhere in the world. New businesses are thriving in sectors unimaginable 20 or so years ago – social networking, sale of content and knowledge, online shopping and take-away food, to name but a few. Even well-established businesses have changed the way they operate and interact with their customers.

These changes are historic, comparable to the impact of exploration of the New World in the late middle ages, or indeed the Industrial Revolution. There are risks – we are all aware of the scares around loss of personal and highly sensitive data by large organisations, disasters impacting data centres, etc.

We all need to be aware of these risks and adapt strategies and processes which will enable us to reduce the likelihood and impact of these risks to acceptable levels.

PREFACE

At my age I don't remember much about my school days. But I do have a very vivid memory of being shown a 35 mm film (yes it was a long time ago) called GIGO – 'Garbage in Garbage Out'. I watched it again recently on YouTube and was struck not only by what had changed so dramatically (no more ticker tape and punched cards) – but also by what had not changed. The risk of programming errors, security and need to change business processes are the same today as they were in 1969 when the film was made. Added to that, we have new risks and challenges with viruses, hackers and advanced persistent threats (APTs), to name a few. The modern information risk manager and auditor needs an appreciation of the whole realm of information risk and governance, in addition to a detailed understanding of their own specialist fields.

I also remember running training in the early 1990s when we stated that by 2002 there would be no computer audit/information risk management (IRM) specialists – all auditors and consultants would have the necessary skills to undertake the work themselves and so specialists would not be required. Thankfully (for me) this has not been the case. The need for IRM specialists/auditors is now greater than ever, as threats have become more complex (e.g. APTs, cyber crime and terrorism). At the same time, the traditional threats still remain and are compounded by general ignorance and naivety of the risks. It is however true that all auditors need an appreciation of the basic information risks facing their organisations and how these can be mitigated.

Preface

The aim of this book is to provide insight and guidance for those considering a career in information risk management, and also to provide an introduction for non-specialists. It has been written in four main parts:

I.   What is risk and why is it important?
     This provides an introduction to general risk management and introduces information risk.

II. Introduction to general IS and management risks
     This gives an overview of general IS controls and the controls over the operation and management of IS. It also considers risks and controls for confidentiality, integrity and availability of information.

III. Introduction to application controls
     This introduces the concepts of application controls, the controls built into systems to ensure that they process data accurately and completely.

IV. Life as an information risk management specialist/auditor
     This provides a guide for those considering, or undergoing, a career in information risk management.

Each chapter contains an overview of the risks and controls that you may encounter when performing an audit of information risk, together with a suggested approach. I have based this approach on risks and controls rather than providing a detailed list of specific questions – given the variety of organisations and technologies in use, I find such questions of very limited benefit unless they are used effectively.

This book is not intended to provide an in-depth analysis – however, there are references to other sources. I hope you find the book helpful, informative and entertaining. Happy auditing.

ABOUT THE AUTHOR

A qualified accountant, Certified Information Systems Auditor and Certified ScrumMaster™, Chris has over 30 years' experience of providing financial and IT advisory and risk management services. He worked for 16 years at KPMG where he managed a number of major IS audit and risk assignments. These included a number of project risk and business control reviews. He was head of information risk training in the UK and also ran training courses overseas including India and throughout mainland Europe. He has worked in a wide range of industry sectors including oil and gas, public sector, aviation and travel.

For the past eight years he has been an independent consultant specialising in financial, SOX and operational controls for major ERP implementations, mainly at oil and gas enterprises.

He is an international speaker and trainer on Agile audit and governance and has published two other titles for ITGP:

1. *Agile Governance and Audit* (2014)
2. *Reviewing IT in Due Diligence* (2015)

x

ACKNOWLEDGEMENTS

Throughout my career I have been blessed with meeting many people who have extended my knowledge and skills – even though in some cases this was as a result of the mistakes that we made together, rather than anything intentional. They were always patient and keen to help me develop my skills – some becoming lasting friends over many years.

I also greatly appreciate the support and advice provided by my friends and former colleagues in the production of this book. In particular, the guidance and support from Diane Hill, Colin Bezant, Scott Nicholls, Mike Hughes, Jackie Price and Manoj Shah – and not forgetting of course the patience and guidance of my wife, Amanda.

As always, I have received great patience and support from the publisher, ITGP, particularly from Vicki Utting and Sophie Sayer. Also to their reviewers, Antonio Velasco and Maarten Souw, for their valuable advice and guidance.

CONTENTS

Contents

Contents

PART I: WHAT IS RISK AND WHY IS IT IMPORTANT?

CHAPTER 1: RISKS AND CONTROLS

Overview

Before considering information risk, we need to understand the basic concepts of risks and how they can be managed. This will put the management of specific IT risks into context and also improve our communication with other risk management professionals. Following financial and other business scandals and crises, there has been an increased focus on risk – a whole industry has been created around the Sarbanes-Oxley Act, impacting US based companies. It has also become an area for academics and standard setters.

In this chapter we will consider:

- What is risk?
- Management of risk
  o Risk awareness and identification
  o Assessing and monitoring risk
  o Responding to risk.

At the end of the chapter there is a summary of the key points.

What is risk?

Risks are all around us. They are part of everyday life – whether we are walking to the shops or climbing Mount Everest. When the first caveman left the shelter of the cave there was a risk of accident, or wild animals, or even other cavemen. We deal with risks all of the time, often without even thinking about them. Some are small – some are huge. There is a saying where I come from that roughly translates as "He who makes no mistakes makes nothing". In other words, without risk there can be no endeavour. Columbus could just have said – "But I might fall off the edge of the world, or die of starvation, or get attacked by wild animals or natives – I think I will stay at home". But instead he weighed the risks, took reasonable steps to reduce them and went anyway. The same could be said of the early IT pioneers. They could have simply decided the risks were too great and just not bothered to invent computers, the Internet, etc. Apple, Facebook and Google are all examples of global IT-based organisations founded by a few people willing to take managed risks.

Risks are not certainties. They may not happen. But if they do, they will have consequences. Take space flight for example, if the early pioneers had sat down and listed all of the things that could go wrong, no one would have left Earth's orbit. Instead, they took a more pragmatic approach, reducing risk where they could, based on their existing knowledge, and then adapting as they learnt lessons and became aware of the major risks.

We could say all new exploration stops (event) because of a fear of risk (trigger) and therefore we do not achieve new inventions or developments (consequence).

Management of risk

Risk management is big business. Consider, for example, the number and size of security companies, health and safety, police, fire, insurance, military, audit and of course information risk specialists. When you look at each of these there are a number of common themes in how they deal with risk:

- Identify threats thereby raising awareness of risk and its consequences.
- Have frameworks for assessing risk.
- Have response mechanisms for reducing risk to an acceptable level.
- Establish monitoring arrangements to see if the risk impacts, or if new risks arise.

Risk identification and awareness

Risk awareness comes from experience and learning. Whenever there is a major disaster we have an opportunity to learn and take different future actions. For example, the sinking of the Titanic led to an awareness of the need for more lifeboats on ships. The discovery that the wrong shaped windows on the Comet aircraft led to metal fatigue when the airframe was under stress, led to fewer air crash incidents.

We all have a different appetite for the risks we are willing to take. If this were not the case, there would be no gambling – as this depends on odds being set based on each of our perceptions of risk and reward. If we all felt the same, we may all want to back the same horse or dog. Or conversely, we could live in a world where everyone gambles recklessly, undertakes dangerous activities without any safety devices, or disappears up the Amazon basin!

In practice, we all have our own level of risk appetite. This will be based on personal experience, our life/financial situation, etc. Unlike risk likelihood/probability and impact it is difficult, if not impossible, to place a metric onto risk appetite. It is a very subjective matter and is not fixed, as it can change as a person or an organisation matures. The risk appetite for an entity will largely be defined from the Board and communicated down. If it is not, the organisation may be taking too little or too much risk to achieve the objectives set by management. Management need to set strategic, financial and operational parameters which provide the decision makers within the organisation with a good steer as to how much risk is acceptable. In addition to experience and situation, external factors will also influence appetite, for example the fiscal and regulatory/ compliance framework the entity operates in, and economic and political factors, will all have an influence. Audit has an important role in challenging management's risk appetite – acting as a check and balance. Similarly, IT audit holds IT management (and the business) to account, in its use of IT.

Documenting risks

There are a number of ways we can state risks. The one I prefer and will use throughout this book, is that something could happen due to an incident that has implications, or:

<Event> <trigger> <consequence>

For example, there is a risk:

- I may get an electric shock ('event') if I put a metal screwdriver into a power socket ('trigger') and so I will die ('consequence'); or

- a hacker could gain access to my bank account ('event') because I am not careful with my passwords ('trigger') and so I will lose most of my savings ('consequence'); or

- I may have a virus on my computer ('event'), if I switch off my antivirus software ('trigger'), and so I could lose my important data and files ('consequence').

Whilst being simple, this approach provides consistency and clarity – the reader can immediately see why the risk is important. I often see risks written as statements, such as:

- Lose customers
- Get prosecuted for health and safety
- Get fined for breaking data protection.

In each of the above examples, the definition is too general; it does not tell why this event may occur, the specific nature of the event, or what will happen as a result. The risk definition should answer the questions 'How?', 'Why?', 'So What?'. It should be brief, no more than a couple of sentences. It should, however, provide enough information to enable analysis and evaluation of the risk.

Some methodologies consider risk as positive as well as negative – i.e. a risk can be an opportunity as well as a threat. When we look at this format <event> <trigger> <consequence> we could apply it to opportunities as well as risks. For example, "If I bet on the 3.30 pm race, the horse I back may win, therefore I will be able to buy myself a treat". Just like risks, there is uncertainty of outcome but we are expressing what could happen.

Within IT projects, risks can be positive as well as negative. For example, if we launch a new website there is a risk that it may be more popular than we expected, leading to a quick return on investment/achievement of business benefits. This may lead to a need to move to the next phase of the website faster than originally intended.

Assessing and monitoring risk

The first consideration is what risks are relevant to the situation being considered. This sounds obvious but I have reviewed many risk frameworks that have simply looked at the wrong risks. The risk may be real but might not have any consequence or specific impact on what we are trying to achieve. For example – the end of the world as we know it could be a real risk. But I don't really need to consider this if I am trying to perform a risk assessment for going to the shops, or launching a new product, or embarking on a new software project.

Risk assessments may be performed at a number of different levels. The Board, or top management of the organisation, for example, may be interested in strategic risks. The finance department will be mainly interested in financial risks. There may be different risks for different operating divisions of the business. There may also be a need to perform a risk assessment for a new project or product being considered for sale. The following techniques can be used in all of these situations.

We all have different perceptions of risk, depending on our experiences and how brave we are. When reviewing risks for an ongoing activity or new endeavour, most organisations will perform a brainstorming workshop – bringing together the main impacted parties. As a risk management professional, you may be called upon to facilitate at such an event. The aim is to allow the discussion of potential risks. It is a cliché but at this stage nothing should be ruled in or out. The facilitator should document all suggestions – no matter how outrageous, as this idea may be a thread leading to a real risk. The best facilitation I ever did was in Flemish and I don't speak a word of it! There was a risk workshop for the audit of an airline – the workshop was a team of Flemish speakers, some of whom found English difficult to work in. So I would introduce a topic and then stand back and let discussion continue. When it went quiet, I asked someone to translate their findings into English, I wrote it down and moved on. The reason it went so well was as a facilitator I could not over influence what was being discussed.

When the list of risks is complete, an assessment of the suggestions can be made. The usual way for a risk assessment is to consider categorisation of the risk, its likelihood and the extent of the potential impact if it does occur. Most organisations will have their own definitions for each of these. I have a given a general overview below.

Categorisation

The common categorisations of risks for organisations are:

- Financial/financial reporting
- Fraud or financial irregularity
- Health and safety
- Going concern/business continuity
- Reputation risk
- Customer impact

- Regulatory or compliance risk
- Strategic risks
- IT and technological risks.

The extent and appetite for each of these risks will depend on the individual organisation. For example, financial reporting risk is very high on the agenda of companies registered on the US stock exchanges, as they need to comply with the Sarbanes-Oxley Act for control over financial reporting. There is also a need for monitoring to ensure that this appetite is not being breached. The following diagram illustrates the top-down direction of the definition and communication of appetite and the reverse bottom-up direction of monitoring.

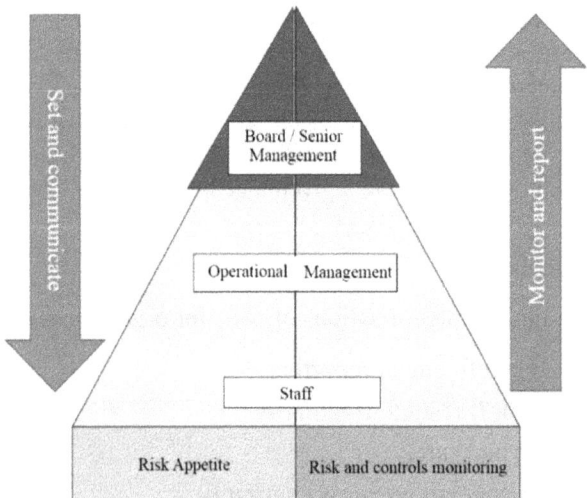

Figure 1: Risk appetite and risk monitoring within an organisation

Likelihood

We need to focus on risks leading to events that are likely to happen. Many organisations have their own categorisations for this. I favour something like Table 1.

Table 1: Assessment of risk likelihood

	Likelihood	Description	Example
5	Almost Certain	Very likely as the event is expected to happen.	We will get rain during winter in London.
4	Likely	There is a strong possibility the event will occur as there is a history of frequent occurrence.	Snow during winter in London.
3	Possible	The event might occur at some time as there is a history of casual occurrence.	1 in 100 years flood in London.
2	Unlikely	Not expected to occur but there's a slight possibility it may.	Earthquake in London.
1	Rare	Could happen, but probably never will, unless we have very exceptional circumstances.	Volcanic eruption in London.

There is a danger that people will always choose the middle option i.e. 'possible' in the above. To get around this, some organisations use an even, rather than odd, number of categories. For example, if we use six categories it forces a decision for a middle grade between three or four, forcing the assessor to decide between 'bad/medium' and 'medium/good'.

If the likelihood is low, it is unlikely to be cost effective to mitigate the risk – the cost of mitigation would be higher than any benefits from resolving it.

Impact

The assessment of impact will depend on the category of risk being considered and the risk appetite of the organisation or business unit. For example, financial risk can be assessed in terms of monetary values, health and safety in terms of incidents/level of injury sustained, etc.

Table 2: Assessment of risk impact

	Description	Financial Impact	Health and Safety
5	Catastrophic	Above £10M	Fatalities or permanent disability or ill-health
4	Major	£5M to £10M	Single death and/or long-term illness or multiple serious injuries
3	Modest	£2M to £5M	Injury; possible hospitalisation and numerous days lost
2	Minor	£300,000 to £2M; not covered by insurance	Minor injury; medical treatment and some days lost
1	Insignificant	Less than £300,000	No or only minor personal injury; first aid needed but no days lost

Unlike the likelihood category, we are able to attach specific values to each category. There is still a highly subjective element in assessing the category for each likely event, but it should be possible to rationalise and document the assumptions that have been made in making the assessment.

Risk heat maps

Having agreed values for the likelihood and impact of each risk, a common way of displaying and comparing the results is to create a matrix in the form of a risk heat map.

Impact	5	High impact/low likelihood	High impact and high likelihood
	1	Low impact and low likelihood	Low impact/high likelihood
		1	5
		Likelihood	

Figure 2: Risk heat map template

Any risks in the top right hand corner will need to be treated as priority. The aim is to introduce mitigations to reduce either the impact or the likelihood of the risk occurring. Typically, organisations will consider their top ten risks and review these on a regular basis to see if there has been any substantial change in risk profile. It is important for the auditor to understand and challenge an organisation's perception of risk and their risk appetite. When an organisation or a project fails, or suffers a major incident, it is often because of a risk that was known about but the likelihood and impact had been underestimated.

One example of this is the risk of mountaineering vs skiing. One of these activities seems inherently more risky than the other. However, the cost of insurance is the same for both – as the chance of an injury or loss of property when skiing is higher than the chance of injury or loss of property when mountaineering, but the impact of the injury/loss is likely to be higher when mountaineering. Our perception is altered by comparing mental/video images of climbers trapped on Mount Everest with advertisements of smiling people on gentle snow-covered slopes.

In the same way, IT organisations are often well protected against the obvious threats but not against those from new/emerging risks and technologies.

Controlling risk

Our human evolution, and indeed our own personal childhood and development, have taught us how to respond to risk. We can run away or avoid a threat ('flight') or alternatively we can conquer the risk by finding a solution ('fight'). By choosing a career in information risk management I have resolved to:

- make management aware of the information risks that are too big to resolve based on our current tools and so need to be avoided.

- help to develop controls and other mitigations which will reduce and monitor risks so that they can be overcome and benefits can be achieved for the organisations we work for.

However, there may still be occasions where the likelihood or potential impact is so small that we choose to 'run away' from the risk, i.e. accept or ignore it.

The level of mitigation needs to be appropriate but not too onerous. I was once asked how much a particular local authority should spend on their disaster recovery arrangements. My answer was that it depended on whether or not they had an incident. If there was an incident, I said they would probably wish they had spent more – if not, they would probably have wished they had spent less. It's the same with any insurance premium. The estimate of likelihood gives an indication, and together with impact, is useful to help assess how much mitigation is required.

There are various ways to remember how to manage risks. They all follow the same terms and one I use is 'TRAIN':

Table 3: Risk treatments

Transfer	Move responsibility to a third party – for example, outsource security, take out insurance, have a disaster recovery service provider.
Reduce	Take pro-active actions to reduce the likelihood or impact. For example, reduce or cease the activity.
Avoid	Avoid the activity so that the risk will not affect us.
Ignore	Accept the risk and continue with the activity. May still include some monitoring to ensure that the risk profile does not change.
Negate (removal)	Changing some aspect of the activity – for example, scope, procurement route, supplier, or sequence of activities. This could include, for example, centralising an activity.

Each of these activities, with the exception of 'ignore', have cost/resource implications and these need to be considered in terms of the cost benefit for the reduction in risk that they could achieve.

If organisations can handle risk, it can give them a competitive advantage over other similar organisations that cannot work at the same level of risk. This is particularly true in information risk management, for example, the development of techniques to authenticate customers has enabled online banking and other commerce whilst not increasing risk.

The key to successful control of risk is to ensure that there is clear ownership and accountability. In many audits I have found it very difficult to identify a specific risk owner who is accountable in this way. A good starting point is to consider the following questions:

- Who would be accountable if the risk became a real business issue?

- Is this clearly understood and communicated?

- Is the control owner fully aware of this responsibility?

- Who would suffer the most?

Summary

Risk and uncertainty about future events is a part of everyday life and in order to thrive and progress we need to be able to handle it in a way that is sensible and not excessive. This depends on the individual or organisation's risk appetite. We need to identify, document (<event> <trigger> <consequence>), assess and manage risks appropriately, particularly those with high potential impact or likelihood. This applies to both positive and negative risks. In order to mitigate and control risks they should be assigned to risk owners.

CHAPTER 2: ENTERPRISE RISK MANAGEMENT (ERM) FRAMEWORKS

Overview

In the last chapter we saw how to identify, assess and report risks at the strategic level. This sets the overall risk context and framework for an organisation. However, if we then try to identify all of the risks at a day to day or operational/tactical level, without reference to this context, there is a danger that:

- the strategic risks may be forgotten or missed, leading to gaps in risk coverage.
- we will be reviewing and mitigating risks that are not significant to the organisation as a whole.

We therefore need a mechanism to connect and synchronise the strategic and operational/tactical risks and controls. This mechanism is often referred to as ERM, or Enterprise Risk Management. In this chapter we will consider:

- What is enterprise risk management?
- Common frameworks for ERM
  - o COSO
  - o ISO31000
  - o Sarbanes-Oxley.
- Summary

At the end of the chapter there is also a summary of key points and take-aways.

What is enterprise risk management?

The phrase enterprise risk management (ERM) has become increasingly popular. It is used to encompass the tools and processes that organisations use to manage risks and ensure that they are making the best use of any opportunities they have to achieve their business objectives. It is important that the information risk management specialist or auditor understands enterprise risk management, as much of their work will need to be in the context of ERM for their entity.

One definition could be:

> *ERM is a <u>strategic enterprise wide</u> management process, to <u>identify potential risks</u> that could <u>significantly impact</u> the entity, and <u>manage them</u> within the entity's <u>risk appetite</u>. The aim is to provide <u>reasonable assurance</u> management can still achieve the entity's strategic objectives.*

Let's look at some of the key elements of this definition in more detail.

Strategic enterprise wide management process

Each operating division, function or geographical market of the business could develop their own approach, tools and processes for risk assessment and management. However, this 'bottom-up' approach has a number of weaknesses, as this approach:

- Will identify risks specific for each location – these may be too granular and of little or no consequence to the organisation as a whole.

- Is expensive to deploy, as resources are required to develop the methodology for each location.
- Is not standard – different levels of effort will be made at each location, probably not related to the overall impact of the risk on the organisation as a whole.
- It will be difficult to consolidate findings for the organisation as a whole and relate them to the strategic business risks.

As a result of the above, enterprise risk management seeks to provide a standardised approach across the enterprise. This will include the tactical and divisional risks within the overall strategic risk management.

Identify potential risks

We could just ask everyone in the organisation to provide a list of risks. This 'bottom-up' approach would provide descriptions of risks that the individual considers to be important (e.g. 'the coffee machine may not work' or 'I am unable to open my office') which whilst important to the individual, are less important to the organisation as a whole. The risk will tend to be operational and tactical rather than strategic. In the early days of SOX implementation, some organisations found themselves with hundreds of risks, only a few of which were relevant to financial reporting and hence the Act.

This approach also leads to duplication and risks that are worded inconsistently, making them very difficult to consolidate and assess at the entity level.

Significant impact

We cannot treat all risks the same – and indeed do not need to. We only need to address those with a potential significant impact. The extent of review and mitigation should be commensurate to the level of risk impact.

Manage them within the entity's risk appetite

COSO's Enterprise Risk Management – Integrated Framework defines risk appetite as follows:

> "The amount of risk, on a broad level, an entity is willing to accept in pursuit of value. It reflects the entity's risk management philosophy, and in turn influences the entity's culture and operating style. ... Risk appetite guides resource allocation. ... Risk appetite [assists the organization] in aligning the organization, people, and processes in [designing the] infrastructure necessary to effectively respond to and monitor risks." – 1 COSO, *Enterprise Risk Management – Integrated Framework*, p. 19.

Each entity will have its own risk appetite, based on history, the sector and business that it operates in. Generally, entrepreneurial organisations would be expected to take more risks because of the greater business opportunities available to them and competition to be the first in the market. Established businesses will take fewer risks because they have more to lose. The appetite for risk should be standard across an organisation and should be 'embedded in its DNA'. If there is too much autonomy for risk the whole business could be brought down by the activities in a particular area.

Enterprise risk management seeks to identify the risk appetite for the entity as a whole and ensure that it is communicated, aligned throughout the entity and complied with via the entities corporate governance framework.

Common ERM frameworks

COSO

The most commonly used and internationally recognised framework is COSO (see *www.coso.org*). The Committee of Sponsoring Organizations of the Treadway Commission (COSO) is a joint initiative to provide thought leadership through the development of frameworks and guidance on enterprise risk management, internal control and fraud deterrence. It was formed in the US after the Treadway Commission issued a report of findings and recommendations in October 1987 – Report of the National Commission on Fraudulent Financial Reporting. It is the framework most commonly used by organisations that have to comply with the Sarbanes-Oxley Act and is also commonly used within the public sector.

COSO provide a wide range of guidance on risk management, etc. The most famous of which is a cube which was updated in 2012. There are a number of critics of COSO citing its complexity and its basis on principles. However, it is still the most widely used and attempts to provide an alternative (e.g. from the Institute of Management Accountants) have generally failed. In my view COSO is a useful tool – like all tools its benefit depends on how it is applied in practice. The following is an overview to give a taste of the framework – further information is widely available on the Internet – including COSO's own website referenced above.

The 'X axis' of the COSOS cube shows <u>three categories</u> (operations, reporting and compliance). Earlier versions had a fourth category, strategic. The 'Y axis' shows <u>five components of ERM</u> (Control environment, risk assessment, control activities, information and communication and monitoring activities. Earlier versions had eight components. The 'Z axis' represents the <u>four levels of an organisation</u> (entity, division, operation and function). The cube structure demonstrates the interaction between the categories, components and levels of an organisation.

The five components

The five risk components form a sequence and are likely to be completed in that order.

1. Control environment

The control environment, sometimes referred to as 'tone at the top', assists the context for the organisation's commitment to control, ethical values and overall integrity. It should be demonstrated through all levels of an organisation, starting with the Board of Directors and their independence and guidance. The Board, or other governance level of an entity, is responsible for evaluation, direction and high-level monitoring of the governance and controls for their entity. The Board should direct the entity's level of control and also ensure adequate monitoring is in place to provide compliance with this agreed control environment.

Under the direction of the Board, management are responsible for planning, building, running and day to day monitoring of the processes of the entity, including governance and risk management/control processes. Management should reflect this with appropriate structures and reporting to ensure that all individuals in the entity are aware of the control environment and that there is a culture to ensure individual accountability for internal control. The IT function is not an exception – it also needs to comply with the control environment by applying the entities' policies, procedures, guidelines and monitoring arrangements to its own controls. We will consider this further in *Chapter 5* (Overview of General IT and Management Risks).

2. Risk assessment

In order to assess risk, the entity first needs to be clear what it is trying to achieve and ensure that this is understood by all. It is then possible to assess the risks relating to these objectives across the entity so that appropriate management arrangements, such as controls, can be introduced. The risk assessment will also depend upon the control environment of the entity, particularly their risk appetite. This will include the risk of fraud or other irregularity and also consider how the risks may change over time.

Risk assessments usually start at the Board and then filter down through all levels of management. Typically, a Board will review the top risks faced on an annual basis using workshops and a risk heat map. As we saw in the last chapter, risk assessment is based on likelihood (or probability) of an event and the likely impact. Any risk assessment for IT needs to follow the same approach and any risks identified should be referenced to the higher level strategic risks.

3. Control activities

Having assessed the risks, it is then possible to select and develop appropriate control activities to reduce the level of risk to a more acceptable level in line with the risk appetite. In the IT context, this could include activities, such as the use of access controls, use of firewalls, or reporting of unauthorised access attempts.

4. Information and communication

The assessment of risk, monitoring of activities, etc. all require the organisation to obtain or generate relevant high quality data or information. Information is also generated internally to ensure all board members and staff are aware of the control environment and their responsibilities. Information risk management specialists or auditors will often be involved in reviewing the accuracy and completeness of this information and the systems and processes by which it is obtained.

5. Monitoring activities

Monitoring activities is important to ensure that we can evaluate the effectiveness of the controls in mitigating risks. This helps to identify gaps or other control failures so that they can be remediated. Monitoring also ascertains whether the components of internal control are present and functioning – across the whole entity. Effective monitoring relies on clear lines of accountability and responsibility, and quality mechanisms to ensure consistency.

Larger organisations will generally use automated tools to ensure that all control activity is monitored on an ongoing basis. This will include a level of control self-assessment and additional independent quality reviews to ensure consistency and integrity of monitoring. Information risk management specialists will be using these tools to monitor their own controls and may also be asked to review the integrity and use of the tool from a technical perspective.

ISO31000

ISO31000 is an international standard for risk management, first published in 2009. The following table will help to compare and contrast ISO31000 with COSO.

Table 4: Comparison of COSO and ISO31000

	COSO	**ISO31000**
Emphasis	Flexible evaluation standard for ERM evaluation	Guidance on risk management process and its implementation
	Describes the 'What'	Describes the 'How'

ISO31000 provides guidelines and principles to help organisations with risk analysis and assessments. It was written to improve risk management techniques and provide better stakeholder confidence in the process. It is most used by organisations new to risk management and can be applied to a wide range of risk management areas, including health and safety and IT. It specifies three main areas for the risk management process to cover:

1. Risk architecture – the roles and responsibilities, communication and risk reporting structures.
2. Risk strategy – the strategy, appetite, attitudes and philosophy as defined in the risk management policy. This will include the objectives that the risk management arrangements are seeking to achieve.
3. Risk protocols – the guidelines specified by the entity, including rules and procedures, methodologies, tools and techniques to be applied. They describe the procedures by which the strategy will be implemented and risks managed.

The above represent the main communication channels within an entity to ensure consistency of risk management.

ISO31000 describes the components of a framework for implementing risk management, including the implementation and ongoing support. There are five main components:

1. Mandate and commitment – conducted by the Board to provide the overall control environment.
2. Design of framework – depends upon the organisation and its context, and includes risk management policy and embedding risk management.

3. Implement risk management – both framework and risk management processes.
4. Monitor and review framework.
5. Improve framework (loops back to 2 above).

Sarbanes-Oxley

Sarbanes-Oxley is not actually a framework in its own right (it is usually used alongside COSO and often COBIT® 5). It has, however, been a great source of work for information risk management specialists since 2002 and so you should know something about it.

It relates to the Sarbanes-Oxley Act 2002, which enforced the establishment of controls, management reporting and independent audit for the financial reporting of any US publicly traded company – including in effect their subsidiaries, even if based outside the US. It is important to emphasise that it only relates to:

* US listed companies, including non-US based operations and subsidiaries but not companies only listed on other stock exchanges (e.g. London).
* Only controls over financial reporting – not other financial controls, or operational controls.
* Usually when SOX is referred to it is in connection with Section 404, which refers to financial reporting.

The Act came about following high-level accounting failures, such as Enron. A way was required to re-establish trust in the financial markets and general financial reporting.

Just after SOX was introduced, it was thought there would be a number of similar initiatives in other areas. Rumours of ESOX (European), and PSOX (public sector) were common. Japan's Financial Instruments Exchange Law (FIEL) requires a management assessment of financial reporting internally and auditors to provide an opinion on this assessment. This is commonly referred to as 'J-SOX', and is applicable to all publicly registered companies on Japanese stock exchanges. It is broadly similar to the SOX requirement described above and the information risk management approach is still applicable.

Summary

The consideration of information risk should not be seen in isolation but in the overall context of enterprise risk management. COSO provides a well-established framework for understanding enterprise risk management and ISO31000 provides guidance on how it can be implemented. For those involved in the specific audit of US registered companies, consideration also needs to be given to SOX and how it impacts their work.

CHAPTER 3: RISK MANAGEMENT ASSURANCE AND AUDIT

Overview

Having established a risk assessment and control framework, the Board/senior management of an organisation will need comfort or assurance that it is designed and operating effectively. To achieve this, as part of their ERM process, many organisations are adopting the three lines of defence model. In this chapter we will consider this model for risk management and compare and contrast internal and external audit roles and responsibilities. Each of these has their own culture, their own roles and responsibilities. As an information risk manager, I have been required to work in all of these capacities. In this chapter we will consider:

- The three lines of defence model
- First line of defence – Business unit staff and management
- Second line – governance, risk and compliance
- Third line – assurance and audit
- Segregation of duties between each line
- Internal vs external audit
- Summary.

Three lines of defence

Everyone within an organisation has some responsibility for governance and control, and this is usually reflected in their terms and conditions of service, or other guidelines that they may be required to adhere to. As a contractor I have often not been allowed on site until I have watched a health and safety video and/or completed a questionnaire. I have also not been allowed access to the client's IT networks until I have completed security training. There is also anti-money laundering, data privacy, restricted exports and anti-bribery training requirements that staff may be required to complete. These responsibilities will apply to staff regardless of which level of defence they are within.

All staff have some responsibility for risk management and compliance. There are staff that will have additional responsibilities for risks, controls and compliance. These can be categorised using the three lines of defence model.

There is increasing criticism of this approach, as some see it as being overly bureaucratic and placing too many restrictions on management's ability to take good risks. My view is that it is a model and needs to be adapted for the benefit of the organisation – this should not prevent management taking decisions that will grow the business but should stop management taking risks beyond the risk appetite of their organisation.

First line of defence – Business unit staff and management

Some staff may have specific controls and risk responsibilities delegated to them, with guidance, training and support, for example:

- Ensuring that activities are in accordance with the organisation's defined and communicated risk appetite (for example, delegated levels of authorisation are not being exceeded, management are aware of any changes to business processes or activities which could impact the level of risk exposure).

- Proposing risk control and mitigation processes for new risk areas.

- Reviewing the impact and likelihood of compliance or regulatory breach for any revised business processes or activities.

- Identifying, assessing and reporting risks.

- Operating specific controls, such as exception reporting, performing checks, reconciling accounts.

- Providing confirmation that controls are operating effectively (controls self-assessment).

- Helping to remediate control deficiencies, including control gaps.

These activities are referred to as the first line of defence. This is the level of primary responsibility for managing risks and controls on a daily basis. To be effective, staff need to be aware of their responsibilities and be given the resources required for the effective operation of activities for these responsibilities. Line managers have responsibility to identify and assess risks and to ensure that adequate controls are in place and are operating effectively. This could include, for example, regular risk assessments (usually annually) and reporting of testing and monitoring of controls (usually quarterly). They also have responsibility for reporting findings, negative and positive, to the next lines of defence.

Generally, information risk managers are unlikely to be employed full time as the first line of defence but there can be exceptions, for example:

- When seconded to the business to help investigate and resolve a specific risk and control problem (e.g. security breaches, implementation of new system).
- When acting in a general management capacity for other IRM specialists (e.g. signing timesheets, completing compliance returns or staff appraisals).

Second line of defence – Governance, risk and compliance

The second line of defence is composed of the entities' own compliance and risk functions. The extent of this activity will depend on the organisation's experience of risk and controls (their control maturity) and also the degree of regulatory control they face. The second line often has its own separate reporting lines into management and is responsible for reviewing risk reports and test evidence produced by the first line. Their main role is to ensure that risks are being managed and reported appropriately. The main activities are:

- Helping the business to produce a realistic and manageable risk appetite and risk strategy.
- Monitoring compliance with regulatory compliance requirements.
- Providing input to maintain and develop risk policies.
- Defining risk and controls processes, reporting frameworks and methodologies, including providing support for automated tools.

- Monitoring and reports on control effectiveness and extent of residual risk.
- Managing risks of IT systems.
- Providing quality assurance function for integrity of compliance data.
- Monitoring relevant regulatory and compliance requirement changes.
- Monitoring execution of change.

Part of the benefit of the second line is that they are, in effect, providing a benchmarking for the organisation, as they are able to oversee the risk and controls management processes for different parts of the business. Increasingly in my experience, the second line is being relied upon by external audit. Many organisations use this as a basis for negotiating lower external audit fees.

The second line of defence is very important as it gives assurance to management and the Board that risk is being managed. For this to be effective, there needs to be clear lines of accountability and responsibility which are defined and understood.

Third line of defence – Independent assurance from audit and the Board

There is a Latin question 'Quis custodiet ipsos custodes?' meaning 'Who will guard the guards?'. Which is often translated today as 'Who audits the auditor?'. This is a good question. In the case of the three lines of defence that will be by audit.

The third line consists of internal audit and possibly the audit committee or other board members. They provide independent validation and assurance over:

- Monitoring of risk appetite and its dissemination through the organisation
- Organisational compliance with delegation of authorities
- Complying with policies
- Appropriateness and compliance with controls and processes
- Proposed changes to methodologies
- Risk reporting framework
- Implementation and data quality of risk reporting
- Assertions of risk exposure
- Implementation of process, policy and control.

The above will include reviews of the first and second lines of defence. To be effective in reviewing IT risks and controls, the internal audit team need to ensure that they have appropriate skills and related resources. This could be achieved via a co-sourcing arrangement.

Segregation of duties between each line

To be effective, the three lines of defence model requires independence of each level. Independence should not only be in practice but also in perception. For example, a husband and wife, or other family members working together, may work with integrity and ensure that there is no conflict – however a third party may believe that such a conflict exists. This alone is often sufficient to reduce faith in the effectiveness of the control. Each level should be independent:

- No-one reviews or audits their own work, transactions or test results.
- No management line conflicts (for example if I was responsible for reviewing the work of whoever set my pay and rations).

Particular care needs to be taken if the boundaries between the levels are blurred. For example, when staff are seconded from internal audit to operational project teams. Employees in the second and third line may also be members of professional bodies with their own codes of conduct for ethics and independence (*see Chapter 11*).

Internal vs external audit

External audit can be either financial audit or certification. Financial external audit is a strict process to provide an opinion on whether the financial accounts provide a true and fair view of the financial history of an entity over the stated financial period.

Internal audit is a function often used by organisations to review the adequacy of their internal controls framework and provide an independent assurance that it is operating effectively. The definition per IIA (Institute of Internal Auditors) is that they:

> "Provide independent assurance that an organisation's risk management, governance and internal control processes are operating effectively."

See *www.iia.org.uk/about-us/what-is-internal-audit/*.

Some organisations also have regular audits conducted by certification auditors (e.g. ISO27001). In addition, outsource providers may be independently audited on behalf of their clients.

It is worthwhile stressing the difference in that external audit's scope is limited to controls over reporting of financial statements, whereas internal audit should consider all IT risks. A failure of a CRM, manufacturing, or supply chain system may not impact the accounts but it can destroy business value quicker than an adverse audit report.

Other forms of IT assurance

Usually as part of the second line of defence, following the implementation of SOX and an increase in general awareness of the need for IT governance, many organisations have introduced additional assurance teams to review key areas of IT risk on a regular basis. The best ones have a wider remit than governance and control – seeking to identify areas of best practice and spread them across the organisation, or to improve processes to make them more efficient and effective.

The main types I have come across are:

- Information security teams – reviewing the policies and standards for IT security, how they are deployed, applied and monitored. Their remit often includes training and awareness, cyber security and fraud and vulnerability detection.

- Data privacy and protection – looking at specific compliance to data protection principles and laws. Can also include policies for definition and compliance of data confidentiality.

- Programme/project risk – reviewing projects and programmes, usually at key stage gates, to ensure compliance with quality standards. May have a significant role in agreeing the Go/No Go decision or criteria to proceed for major projects.

- Data analytics are another emerging form of assurance. For example, organisations are increasingly using big data and analytics engines to identify potential errors in data, to ensure compliance with controls and regulations. Similarly, major banks have automated routines to detect unusual or impossible patterns of expenditure (for example, withdrawing cash from a bank in Alabama at the same time as you buy a train ticket in Swindon will indicate that your bank details have probably been cloned/stolen and they will stop the transaction).

Case study

A large UK organisation that had previously had major financial reporting issues, needed to comply with the Sarbanes-Oxley Act. To ensure compliance they brought in specialists from a number of different accounting, legal and consulting companies. As this was in the early days of SOX, their opinions differed. Also, the companies were reviewing the work of each other, large numbers were attending meetings and the teams provided changed on a regular basis. In addition to generating large costs, this led to confusion and a lack of ownership of governance and control by management.

The organisation adopted the three lines of defence model and clarified the responsibilities of each level. They recruited their own staff into these teams to work alongside the consultants to develop new processes and procedures for reviewing risks, monitoring and testing controls, and compliance and governance reporting. This reduced the costs of compliance, ensured that compliance failures were identified and resolved quickly and ensured consistency across the group. The approach also identified areas for process and control standardisation, leading to reduced operating costs.

Summary

Having established a risk management framework, organisations need to ensure it is working effectively. The three lines of defence model helps with this. We have seen that information risk management auditors and consultants may work in a number of different areas of an organisation. Their focus is always to ensure that the organisation is aware of risks and is taking reasonable steps to mitigate the risks. There is a need for ongoing review and reporting as the threat landscape will change over time.

CHAPTER 4: INFORMATION RISKS AND FRAMEWORKS

Overview

So far we have considered the nature of risk and how it impacts organisations. As information is a key asset of an organisation, a significant area of investment, and one with specific risk implications, it should be high on the agenda of most organisations. Much mystique has arisen around IT assurance because of its technical nature – however, the basic principles are the same as for any other risk impacting the entity. In this chapter we will consider:

- What is information risk?
- The frameworks to help analyse and manage risk:
  - o COBIT 5
  - o ISO standards
  - o CRAMM.
- Summary

Management frameworks, such as PRINCE2® and ITIL® will be considered later in the book in the relevant chapters. Other frameworks are available, for example the Project Management Body of Knowledge (see *www.pmi.org*).

What is information risk?

To fit into the overall enterprise risk management for an entity, any risks for information should relate to the overall business risks. For example, we could consider the risk of penetration of websites; however, this needs to be seen in the context of the related business risk of loss of customer data or intellectual property of the company. We could consider the need for a disaster recovery plan for a computer centre – but this needs to be seen in the context of overall business recovery in the event of an incident. In my opinion, there are no such things as IT risks. Instead, we have risks to the business that have IT causes or consequences. In other words, we only need to consider IT risks if there is a potential business impact. This is a useful sense check to apply.

So what is different about IT risks? The main difference is their pervasive nature increases the level of impact. For example, access to one system can give access to all data and services.

A common mnemonic for summarising IT risks is 'CIA' which has been in use for some time now. It is mainly used in the context of security risks and controls, however I find it a useful way to assess risks for any IT scenario. CIA stands for:

Confidentiality

Integrity

Availability

Management is sometimes also added as a fourth factor.

Confidentiality relates to data security and privacy. It is about ensuring that data is not lost or disclosed in an unauthorised way. This could be due to physical security, such as leaving a laptop on a train, or allowing unauthorised visitors, or not physically securing laptops to the desk with suitable devices. It could also be due to poor logical security, such as poor passwords, not using screensavers to time out, failing to encrypt key data sent in emails, or poor website and firewall controls. The consequences of any loss of data could include loss of reputation, compliance fines and prosecutions, loss of customers, or loss of intellectual property assets. With Internet fraud on the increase, data has a value and there have been cases of very large amounts of personal employee data or credit card information being traded. We will consider data confidentiality and privacy further in *Chapter 7*.

Integrity in the security sense applies to preventing data from being changed by unauthorised persons. Legitimate users of data need to have comfort and assurance that the data they use is accurate and complete. I was in a restaurant once and left a tip of £12 on a bill of £120. The restaurant entered it incorrectly (after I had verified the transaction) and a few days later I received a call from my credit card company saying that there was a large/unusual transaction. The tip had been entered as £12,000! These sorts of errors should not occur.

To me integrity is about more than security. From an IT controls perspective it also includes the integrity of systems and processes that amend data. Therefore, I also consider the following under integrity:

- Change control processes for systems should ensure that full testing of changes is made prior to them being implemented in a live environment (see *Chapter 7*).
- Governance and other controls in the system development lifecycle for projects and programmes to produce new systems (also see *Chapter 7*).
- Data processing controls, for example to ensure that interfaces and batch processes are run completely, timely and accurately (see *Chapter 9*).

- Controls within applications to ensure that all transactions produce accurate, complete and reliable results. This may include validation of data entered via screens, or management information to monitor the output of key processes (also *Chapter 9*).

Availability in the IT security context relates to ensuring that authorised users, etc. can access information when it is needed. The main availability security risks are preventing denial-of-service attacks (DoS). Downtime of key websites could be extremely costly to reputation and loss of business if customers are unable to place orders online. Availability can also be lost through physical incidents, such as power loss, floods, fire or even pestilence! The following examples are all cases I have come across:

- Computer and communications suite located below ground level and under the works canteen (the IT staff entered the room in wellington boots after the inevitable flood from the kitchen).
- Smoking being allowed in a room on the same air conditioning circuit as the computer suite (the director's pipe set off the system and flooded the room).
- Computer situated under a flat roof that leaked (the mainframe had a plastic sheet over it).
- Main computing centre for a US based company was on top of the San Andreas Fault. Another centre was in a hurricane zone.

The main ways to ensure availability are to build in resilience, such as alternate processing capabilities and ensuring data is regularly and fully backed up and stored offsite.

I also include the ability to respond and resolve small incidents as part of availability. To a user the availability relates to the systems and data they want to use. Hence if there is a problem with a particular application, this can have as big an impact to some users as the whole system being unavailable.

A comprehensive and regularly tested disaster recovery plan is also vital.

We will consider these issues further in *Chapter 8*.

The management of IT can also be a risk area. IT represents a large investment. There is also an increasing trend for bring your own devices (BYOD) and other DIY approaches, which whilst they may be appropriate for domestic use and reduce costs of delivery, do reduce the level of control an organisation has over its own IT. For example, I know of one company where staff felt that the IT support they received from the service desk provider was too slow and ineffective. There were a couple of people on the factory floor who therefore decided to fix the problems themselves. This included introducing software to identify and fix problems, which unknown to them contained viruses.

Management risks of IT include:
- Poor administration or governance of the service (see *Chapter 5*).
- Lack of strategic direction for the development of the service and IT investment – failure to provide what the business needs now or in the future.
- Poor control over third parties providing IS services.

The CIA (M) mnemonic is very useful – I have used it in interviews as well as in reviewing new client situations.

COBIT 5

COBIT 5 (originally known as Control Objectives for Business and Information Technology – now just known by the acronym) is the latest version of a series of tools developed by ISACA (originally known as the Information Systems Audit and Control Association, but now just known by the acronym). COBIT is a valuable toolkit for information risk management, as it provides a structure and guidance for a number of the reviews that IRM specialists are likely to be asked to perform. Many of the tools are available free of charge to ISACA members – or can be purchased on licence from ISACA for reasonable fees (see *www.isaca.org/COBIT*). ISACA describe COBIT 5 as *"The only business framework for the governance and management of enterprise IT"*. The tool is available as an online version or as a series of guides. At the time of writing the tool is useable, however additional features and documents are planned to be added in due course. I have listed below some of the main publications available:

- A Business Framework for the Governance and Management of Enterprise IT
- COBIT 5 Enabler Guides (see *www.isaca.org*)
- COBIT 5 Professional Guides (see *www.isaca.org*).

The ISACA website also provides other tools to assist with assessments, laminate summaries and conversion from earlier versions of COBIT. The tool is used very widely internationally, often adapted for use within specific organisations. Training and certification in its use is also available.

The tool is extremely sophisticated and contains many elements. The easiest way to get an overview is to read *A Business Framework for the Governance and Management of Enterprise IT* (see *www.isaca.org*). This includes:

- A summary of the framework documents
- An introduction to information governance
- Descriptions for the five principles in COBIT 5:
  Principle 1: Meeting stakeholder needs
  Principle 2: Covering the enterprise E2E
  Principle 3: Applying a single integrated framework
  Principle 4: Enabling an holistic approach
  Principle 5: Separating governance from management.

These principles place information governance in a firm context within ERM (*see previous chapter*). The guide provides more details on each of the steps and identifies 37 governance and process areas:

Table 5: COBIT 5 Summary of process areas

Activities	Number of processes	Example of processes
Evaluation, direction and monitoring (Governance)	4	Ensure benefit delivery
Align, plan and organise (Mgt)	13	Manage service agreements
Build, acquire and implement (Mgt)	10	Manage configuration
Deliver service and support	6	Manage operations
Monitor, evaluate and assess MEA	3	MEA of system of internal control

The framework document:

- provides guidance for the implementation of COBIT 5, including making a business case.

- outlines the process capability model.

- provides supporting appendices, including mapping of COBIT 5 to the ISO/IEC 38500 framework.

Knowing about security does not make you a good auditor – you also need other skills and tools. COBIT can provide a structure and framework to help. There are also mappings for COBIT 5 to ISO27001.

Whilst COBIT 4 is no longer supported, you may find it still in use at some organisations that prefer the older style presentation based on control objectives.

ISO frameworks

ISO (International Organization for Standardization) is an independent, non-governmental membership organisation based in Geneva who develop voluntary International Standards. These standards provide globally accepted specifications for products, services and systems. Compliance is often requested in international contracts, including for outsourced IT services. ISO has published over 19,500 International Standards covering almost every industry, including technology.

The main standards of relevance to information risk management are:

- ISO31000 – Risk management (*see Chapter 2*)

- ISO27001 – Information security (*see Chapter 6*)

- ISO22301 – Business Continuity (*See Chapter 8*).

CRAMM

The IT Infrastructure Library promoted the CCTA Risk Analysis and Management Method (CRAMM). I have not seen this methodology used recently but it may still be in circulation so I have included it for completeness. CRAMM was a software tool with a number of associated useful templates and tools, requiring heavy training of users. It used templates to capture and assess risks in a structured way and then enabled management of these through mitigations. There were three main stages:

1. Identification and valuation of assets
2. Threat and vulnerability assessment
3. Countermeasure selection and recommendation.

Summary and key take-aways

The use of CIA (**C**onfidentiality, **I**ntegrity and **A**vailability) provides a good way to summarise IT and information risks and provides a basis for audit and assessment. There are also a number of useful internationally recognised standards and policies that the IRM specialist must be aware of, the main ones being COBIT 5 and ISO27001.

PART II: INTRODUCTION TO GENERAL IT AND MANAGEMENT RISKS

CHAPTER 5: OVERVIEW OF GENERAL IT AND MANAGEMENT RISKS

Overview

IT controls are composed of:

- controls specific to individual systems (referred to as 'application controls') and

- those controls common across the whole organisation, division of computer platform (referred to as 'IT general controls').

Both operate within the overall context of entity level controls:

- Entity level controls are about the tone and culture of the organisation.

- IT general controls are those within the IT management processes to provide a reliable and appropriate operating environment and support the effective operation of application controls.

Application controls will be covered in a later chapter.

To put this in another way, IRM is a group of closely related specialties that can be summarised in addressing the following:

- Is the data asset collated, inputted and changed accurately and completely? (application controls).

- Are IT and information operations well organised to ensure data safety and security? (operational controls).

- Does the process of acquiring new software and ensuring business change guarantee that information applications continue to support the operations and long term objectives of the organisation? (Programme and project controls).

A review of entity and general IT controls is a good starting point for the IRM auditor/reviewer if they are undertaking a range of audits. Not only will it set the context, but it will also provide an opportunity to understand the culture and IT risk profile of the organisation. It also provides an opportunity to gather information to be used on other IT audits, such as an inventory of systems, locations of data processing sites, extent of outsourcing and organisation and reporting charts.

General IT controls relate to more than one application. In this chapter we will consider:

- Reviewing entity level controls in an IT context
- What are general IT controls?
- Requirements for reviewing infrastructure and environmental controls
- Summary and key take-aways.

Reviewing entity level controls in an IT context

Entity level controls apply to all aspects of an organisation's operations, including information technology. Typically they will include:

- Business strategies and plans
- Risk assessment activities

- Policies, procedures and other communicated guidelines
- Training and education
- Quality assurance
- Compliance (e.g. health and safety, data protection and specific industry or fiscal requirements)
- Quality assurance and internal audit.

The review of entity level controls will usually be outside the remit of an information risk manager and will be undertaken by a general auditor. There may be occasions, however (e.g. when undertaking an independent audit of an outsource provider), where the information risk manager wishes to gain an understanding of the context in which controls operate. When reviewing entity level controls we will be looking for the definition and publication of information about:

- The allocation of accountabilities and responsibilities for governance, risk and general management of the IT function (for example, does the Board consider information and information security issues?).
- Production and publication of policies and supporting guidance – including policy around the security of information and safeguarding of IT assets. These policies can be vital if there are irregularities. For example, if a member of staff transfers all of their business emails to their personal email address, this could be seen as normal behaviour unless this is expressly forbidden in policies and in terms and conditions of employment – in such cases it may be difficult or impossible to bring disciplinary actions.

- Monitoring of governance and control, including internal audit. This includes the governance, control and internal audit of IT. For example, is there the capability and technical competence to provide governance and internal audit of IT functions?
- Financial and other reporting.
- The link between business strategy and IT strategy. Given the pervasiveness of IT in modern business, if the two are not properly aligned, especially to ensure the IT strategy is aligned to the business strategy but also so that the business understands how IT can enable it, then it's likely that there will be other underlying IT control failings. Also, it is unlikely in these situations that IT will deliver solutions that meet the business needs – which will have a consequent impact on controls.
- Organisation's risk appetite.

The above will apply to all aspects of an organisation. From an information risk perspective they also enable us to understand what the attitude and approach to information security will be.

In summary, we would expect there to be specific considerations, for example:

- Policies and procedures for information security, data confidentiality and protection (for example, as illustrated by new starter packs)
- Board interest and involvement in cyber security initiatives
- Commitment to change control and system development controls and processes

- Internal audit coverage of all aspects of IT risk and control.

The auditor will need to obtain evidence that all of the entity level controls operate as described. This could include interviewing the Board/internal audit/line staff or reviewing board minutes and documentation of sign offs of acceptance of security policies.

The classification in the IT Governance Institute paper *IT Control Objectives for Sarbanes-Oxley 2006*, although based on the previous version of COBIT (4.1), provides a useful categorisation of areas to consider using the COSO framework as a basis. This provides a useful checklist of questions for those new to IRM auditing, even if their organisation is not required to comply with SOX.

What are general IT controls?

General IT controls are pervasive controls and by considering centrally, where possible, we do not then have to consider them individually for every application. They relate to the environment surrounding the information application systems.

Once again the IT Governance Institute paper *IT Control Objectives for Sarbanes-Oxley 2006,* although based on the previous version of COBIT (4.1), provides a useful categorisation of areas to consider.

Table 6: Summary of COBIT 4 objectives for SOX

Control Objective area (COBIT 4)	Risk	Expected controls
Acquire and Maintain Application Software (AI2)	Application software does not meet the business requirements.	• SDLC methodology • Post implementation reviews
Acquire and Maintain Technology Infrastructure (AI3)	IT infrastructure is not appropriate for business requirements and systems in place.	Procedures for acquiring technology and attaching to network
Develop and Maintain Policies and Procedures for acquisition and development (various)	Inconsistent or inappropriate software and infrastructure in place.	Policies and procedures for development, change, etc.
Install and Test Application Software and Technology Infrastructure (AI7)	Inadequate testing prior to being placed in production, causing malfunctions and inaccurate or incomplete data.	• Testing strategy including load and functionality, data conversion • Change management controls for loading into production

Control Objective area (COBIT 4)	Risk	Expected controls
Manage Changes (AI6, AI7)	Unauthorised changes made to production systems introducing error or other irregularity.	• Change management process including authorisations, emergency change requests • Access controls to prevent unauthorised loading into production • Risk assessment of new software or patch updates
Define and Manage Service Levels (DS1)	The level of service may not be appropriate for the requirements of the business – leading to inadequate level of performance or excessive costs.	• Service level agreements/contracts • Performance and capacity monitoring and reporting

Control Objective area (COBIT 4)	Risk	Expected controls
Manage Third-Party Services (DS2)	Services provided by third parties may not be as secure, accurate or available as they would be if provided in house.	• Contract in place and performance monitored • Regular, independent monitoring and review • Confirmation of competence to provide service • Access rights to inspect operation
Ensure Systems Security (DS5)	Unauthorised use, disclosure, change or loss of data leading.	• Information security policies and plans • Security standards, training and awareness • Procedures to authenticate and review users • Procedures for establishing, changing and removing user access rights • Physical and environmental controls (e.g. locks, CCTV).

Control Objective area (COBIT 4)	Risk	Expected controls
Manage the Configuration (DS9)	IT components may not be protected to prevent unauthorised changes.	• Restrict users to authorised software • Firewalls, etc. • Access based on need • Antivirus protection • Configuration checked against approved configuration design
Manage Problems and Incidents (DS8, DS10)	Inappropriate identification, recording, response and resolution of incidents causing loss of service or unidentified risks of unauthorised access/error.	• Incident and problem management process • Audit trail and other reporting of incident handling • Hands-off to disaster recovery management
Manage Data (DS11)	Data may not be complete, accurate, timely and valid throughout the processing cycle.	• Data distribution, storage and retention policies • Protection of sensitive data • Backup arrangements • Tested ability to recover backed-up data • Change control for data structures

Control Objective area (COBIT 4)	Risk	Expected controls
Manage Operations (DS13)	Systems may not be running as planned causing synchronisation or other errors.	• Operations procedures and policies • History logs retained

The risks are common but the likelihood and potential impact for each will vary depending on the entity concerned. Most organisations will have a single or limited number of common controls for each of the above.

Case studies and examples of general IT controls

Examples of poor physical security/environmental controls

- An organisation had taken great care to ensure its main computer room was safe from external flooding as it was slightly below ground level. Unfortunately they forgot it was located below the staff restaurant kitchen – which flooded one night causing extensive damage and disruption.

- Another organisation had a mainframe computer situated beneath a flat roof – this leaked with similar consequences to the above (despite computer operations staff efforts to cover it with a plastic sheet).

- It was a hot summer weekend. Some maintenance work was being performed at a site that had strong security. Because of the heat the workforce wedged a back door open with a fire extinguisher and then

> went to lunch at the local hostelry. When they came
> back they found that thieves had entered the
> building and removed desktops, laptops, etc.
>
> ### *Which one shall I use?*
>
> All I wanted was a copy of the IT security policy. I
> asked and was given four completely different
> documents, in different styles and in one case with
> conflicting content. All claimed to be the organisation's
> official version. We took the best from each document
> and had a new version approved and issued. There
> cannot be a consistent approach to IT security and
> control without a standard single baseline, with clear
> lines of ownership and responsibility for update.

Outsourced arrangements

The IRM auditor may be asked to review arrangements
for the outsourcing or off-shoring of IT services. The
lifecycle can be summarised as follows:

- Definition of requirements
- Design of solution
- Management of arrangements
- Ongoing review.

The most common area for such involvement is during the
manage phase – for example, to conduct a review at the
service provider site, or review the adequacy and
relevance of any independent audit. Such an audit will
have been completed by an independent auditor to an
International Standard, such as ISAE3402 (formally

known as a SAS70 type II review). The International Standard on Assurance Engagements (ISAE) No. 3402, Assurance Reports on Controls at a Service Organization, was introduced in June 2011 (see *www.ifac.org*).

The independent audit should include testing and provide a report which the clients of the service provider can rely upon, rather than having to perform their own review. As well as being less disruptive to the service provider (and saving their carpets being worn out from constant audits!), it is more convenient for clients – particularly if the service is provided from a different country. When client organisations rely upon these audits, they need to ensure that the scope of the audit covers the locations, processes and controls that are relevant for that organisation. There should still be the right for a client's own inspection/audit visit to the site if this is necessary.

Outsourcing takes many different forms; it started with services, but is increasingly found to be specific to infrastructure, or process as a service. Examples include:

- Infrastructure as a service – a data centre is outsourced to a third party.
- Process as a service – the supply chain is outsourced to a third party logistics provider – so you provide them with inventory and order data and they provide you with information around fulfilled orders.
- Software as a service – you use a Cloud based software package where the supplier controls the code and automatically pushes through updates.
- Third party applications on mobile devices that you incorporate as part of your overall process.

Not all of these services will have an ISAE3402 report, so it is really important for the organisation to understand who has responsibility for controls and how to evidence IT controls across this landscape. Otherwise failure of one component may have an impact on the whole. It can help to take a systems landscape diagram and overlay that with who is responsible for controls (IT, supplier, don't know!) for each of the applications/services on the landscape.

End user computing

Users are provided with very powerful tools by their employers and are able to tailor applications to their own requirements. The most commonly used and powerful tools are spreadsheets – particularly MS Excel. These enable users to perform very complex operations. Whilst many users have a very advanced knowledge of how to use these tools, less have the knowledge of how to do so in a secure way which ensures the integrity of the data being processed. I have been involved in a number of situations where decisions were made based on erroneous spreadsheets, or where confidential data had been released by mistake in emails (usually hidden in a workbook when the user just wanted to send the first worksheet in the workbook).

For higher risk end user computing, for example where it impacts financial reporting, or key decisions based on models – for example mergers and acquisitions, we would expected additional controls to be in place including:

- End user policies and procedures implemented and circulated to relevant teams

- Documentation standards, including the need for embedded controls to ensure sort, summarise and perform calculations/reporting

- Appropriate access and backup arrangements (including guidance on use of PC based and detachable storage drives)

- Verification (e.g. peer review or the use of automated tools) to confirm integrity of processing.

Bring your own devices (BYOD)

To reduce costs and also to allow for the personal technology preferences of their staff, many organisations are now allowing staff to bring their own devices for use at work. The controls we would expect include:

- Policies and procedures covering use of BYOD (some organisations have a total ban – others have a restricted policy). I have found a number that still have no policy.

- Arrangements for firewall or similar control of areas on the tablet, phone or other device. These may include arrangements to clear these areas automatically if the user is no longer an employee.

Case studies and examples of outsourcing

A large SOX multinational service based organisation was seeking to reduce its management costs and so outsourced its application development and maintenance activity to a service provider. I was asked to undertake a review of the arrangements and help to design a control framework suitable after the transition. We were able to:

- specify the control requirements and ensure these were included in the contract and service levels.
- design monitoring and access arrangements.
- create a framework for ongoing monitoring of controls.

The transition was made successfully.

Reviewing general IT controls

An audit or review of general IT controls is likely to include:

- an assessment of the specific risks for the organisation and location (probably based on confidentiality, integrity and availability).
- enquiries of management to ascertain arrangements to mitigate these risks.
- review of the following as applicable.

System development and program change (Integrity)

- SDLC methodology and process
- Examples of post implementation reviews
- Procedures for acquiring technology and attaching to network
- Policies and procedures for development, change, etc.
- Testing strategy including load and functionality, data conversion

- Change management controls for loading into production
- Change management process including authorisations and emergency change requests
- Access controls to prevent unauthorised loading into production
- Risk assessment of new software or patch updates.

IT operations (Integrity)

- Service level agreements/contracts
- Performance and capacity monitoring and reporting
- Contract in place and performance monitored
- Configuration checked against approved configuration design
- Incident and problem management process
- Audit trail and other reporting of incident handling
- End user computing
- Bring your own device policies.

Outsourced service

- Evidence of regular, independent monitoring and review
- Confirmation of competence to provide service (e.g. ISAE3402 or similar report, ISO certifications and evidence of audit)
- Evidence of access rights to inspect operation.

Access and security controls (Confidentiality)

- Information security policies and plans
- Security standards, training and awareness
- Procedures to authenticate and review users
- Procedures for establishing, changing and removing user access rights
- Evidence of physical and environmental controls (e.g. locks, CCTV).
- Evidence of antivirus protection
- Data distribution, storage and retention policies
- Backup process documentation and examples of logs
- Evidence of testing of recovery backed-up data
- Operations procedures and policies
- Examples of system history logs.

Summary

For information risk management specialists/auditors new to an organisation, a review of general IT controls is a useful starting point, as it provides an overview of the controls in place and the culture for IT governance. It also does not require any specific application process knowledge or experience. General IS controls should provide a firm foundation for other system controls. For example:

- Controls to ensure that only permitted users can perform certain levels of transactions, say over $5000, will only be effective if, for example:
  - o There are policies and procedures in place to make staff aware of these controls

- o General access controls ensure that only authorised managers can give the transaction authorisation to staff
- o Program codes cannot be changed unless authorised.
- Errors and exceptions can be identified and corrected only if, for example:
  - o There is correct routing of reports
  - o There is a clear culture to ensure that errors are resolved
  - o Unauthorised changes cannot be made to the underlying programs or date.

Good general IT controls ensure that these risks have been identified and that suitable mitigations have been identified, implemented and that their effectiveness is regularly monitored.

CHAPTER 6: SECURITY AND DATA PRIVACY

Overview

There is increasing awareness in the media and elsewhere of cyber terrorism and cyber crime. These are very real risks. Less publicised are the internal risks of data loss – through deliberate action or simple carelessness/lack of understanding of the risks. I like ISACA's definition of information security. It defines information security as something that:

> "Ensures that within the enterprise, information is protected against disclosure to unauthorised users (confidentiality), improper modification (integrity) and non-access when required (availability)."

This definition clearly makes it the responsibility of the organisation to protect its information, in the same way as it would any other asset and clearly defines loss in this context.

The area of IT/information security is one where much has been written and it is not my intention to give a full or technically detailed account. What I can do is to give you the basics so that you can conduct an audit or review. For example, you may need to know the distinction between information security and IT security, as these two terms are often confused. Information security looks at all information whether processed manually or on IT systems, whilst IT security addresses the specific technology controls required to support information security.

Many IRM specialists specialise in this single field – why? Because it represents the main area people think of in information risk. There are so many media articles about hacking cases, threats from governments or terrorist organisations, etc. There are also data privacy regulations to consider and initiatives, such as cyber security. The IRM audit specialist needs a basic understanding of the concepts of IT and information security and often sits as an interpreter or go between, bringing the deeper security specialists together with the rest of the business. Whilst the technical aspects can be very involved, IT security is not just about ticking checklists – it's about changing behaviours and culture so that users are aware of the potential for phishing/social engineering and the need to act as the first line of defence against potential threats and vulnerabilities.

Like all areas of information risk, it should start with a consideration of risks and controls and then develop into how we approach our audit.

Risks

A review of IT security often starts at the technical level. In my opinion it is better to start at the business level. Why do we want to keep our information confidential?

- Risk of financial loss if transactions are intercepted (direct and indirect risk).

- Embarrassment and loss of reputation (including future business prospects) if data is revealed.

- Fines or other sanctions from non-compliance with data privacy legislation or regulations.

Each organisation will have different threats and vulnerabilities. This will partly depend upon their choice of technologies, their profile (some business areas are higher risk than others) and culture/security awareness. It is hence necessary to conduct a specific risk assessment for each organisation.

Controls

The main types of control are summarised below:

Security principles and policies

These set out the organisation's risk appetite for loss of information and are expressed in business rather than technical language. The policies will vary between organisations but will generally include data classification, information security, data protection/privacy, acceptable use, data retention and incident management.

Governance and management processes

Provides tools and processes to enact the policy. The UK Government's Cyber Essentials scheme identifies five key controls that all organisations should have as a minimum:

1. Boundary firewalls and Internet gateways – can effectively restrict access to or from networks if properly configured and maintained.
2. Secure configuration – ensuring systems are configured in a secure way. Examples include use of single sign on and development of specific user profiles restricted to the user's legitimate need. This could, for example, include the lockdown of PCs to

prevent use of USB drives or other media that could be used to copy and remove data from the organisation's network.

3. Access control – to ensure only authorised users have access and then only to the data specified for their use by the security configuration.
4. Malware protection – ensuring that virus and malware protection is deployed, installed and used.
5. Patch management – ensuring that software used is the latest supported versions with up-to-date security patches provided by the vendor.

Culture, ethics and behaviour

Tools and processes alone are not enough. If the culture does not drive correct behaviours, users will quickly find dangerous workarounds that will leave systems vulnerable to attack. There are some very effective ideas for communicating the expected culture and behaviours – including screensavers, life-size cardboard statues and stickers for laptops.

Examples of IT security controls

Some examples of basic IT security controls are as follows:

- Access controls – approval (processes to ensure that users are approved to access information resources), authorisation (ensuring access permissions are defined) that systems are configured to provide the right level of access (least privilege, need to know and SoD being considered), authentication (ensuring that when users access an information resource we can authenticate that they are indeed that person through user ID and password controls, biometrics, certificates, etc.).

- Network controls – firewalls, routers, etc. (secure configuration for boundary and internal network protection), network design (segregation of networks, use of DMZs, remote access methods), wireless network security (ensuring wireless devices are configured securely and that rogue wireless networks are detected and removed).

- Application and system development – ensuring that security is built into the development lifecycle and design of any software (e.g. input, validation and output controls, protection of web-based applications (see OWASP), secure coding), ensuring systems are tested before being implemented, ensuring code is safely stored (e.g. in escrow or backed up), segregating development and live environments.

- Vulnerability management – ensuring antivirus and malware protection is installed on all hosts and end point devices, preventing unauthorised mobile code from running, such as ActiveX or Java, ensuring systems are securely configured to approved standards (e.g. NIST, CIS, etc.), ensuring patch management is regularly performed and that software versions are kept current.

- Physical security – ensuring that physical access (secure facility, cameras, etc.) and environmental controls (fire and flood prevention, UPS, etc.) are in place at hosted or internal computer room sites.

- Communications security – use of encryption where information classification requires so either at rest or in transit, protection of email outbound and inbound, restrictions or protection over Internet usage.

- Monitoring controls – logging and review of security events, monitoring network device activity (IDS/IPS), regular monitoring of users and associated access permissions, monitoring of email usage, log in banners which inform users that monitoring may be performed.

- Incident management – defining how incidents will be identified, recorded, handled and escalated, linkage into IT service continuity processes.

- IT availability and service continuity – understanding recovery times for systems and ensuring that systems are built with redundancy and resilience, reducing single points of failure, backup facilities, hot sites and failover solutions, defining disaster recovery plans and testing them, integration of DR plans into BCPs.

ISO27001

The ISO27001 series consists of:

> ISO/IEC 27001:2013
> Information technology – Security techniques – Information security management systems – Requirements
>
> ISO/IEC 27002:2013
> Information technology – Security techniques – Code of practice for information security controls
>
> ISO/IEC 27003:2010
> Information technology – Security techniques – Information security management system implementation guidance

ISO/IEC 27004:2009
Information technology – Security techniques – Information security management – Measurement

The main standard, 27001, covers:

- Organisational context
- Leadership
- Planning
- Support
- Operation
- Performance evaluation
- Improvement.

The standard is highly popular and widely used. Organisations can obtain certification to the standard. Some information risk managers obtain qualification and provide audit of 27001.

Case study examples

> *Help (yourself) desk*
>
> At one organisation I phoned the helpdesk with an issue and was asked to provide my access ID and password – I refused. This request was in contravention of the organisation's security policy.

> **Who would have guessed it?**
>
> In the days before passwords were encrypted, I was helping to implement a new system and decided to check the password file. I found the passwords were 'Newt', 'Frog', 'Toad' and 'Tadpole'. There was obviously some disclosure amongst the four members of staff in this team and so I made them change the passwords and checked a week later. I found the passwords were now 'Robin', 'Thrush', 'Blackbird' and 'Sparrow'. Easily guessable passwords are as worthless as if they were written down.

Documenting, assessing and testing security and confidentiality controls

- Review the risk assessment for IT security to ensure that it is up to date for current threats facing the organisation.

- Review policies and principles to ensure they cover all of the identified security risk areas and are up to date and approved. It is also worth checking that they have been circulated and that staff are aware of them. Most organisations now require a formal sign-off of acceptance from all new members of staff and higher risk organisations also require an annual renewal of this acceptance.

- Identify the tools and processes in place, including for the five major cyber security controls. Review arrangements for ensuring that these are up to date and deployed and operating effectively.

If all of the above show that controls are generally adequate, I may then consider requesting a more detailed specific IT security audit from an appropriate specialist – for example penetration testing, firewall security, etc.

Summary

IT security is a highly specialised area. However, there are a number of checks that any IRM auditor can perform to assess whether their organisation has the basic starting components to address risk.

CHAPTER 7: SYSTEM DEVELOPMENT AND CHANGE CONTROL

Introduction

All computers need software – apps or systems, or programs – in order to be of use. Some are hidden and work in the background (for example to print a document), others we call and use as we need them (e.g. payroll packages, games or social media apps). Some allow for tailoring by the user, or enable us to write our own 'software' in the form of databases or spreadsheets, for example.

Whatever the source and type, we place a lot of trust in their ability to do what we want – to provide reliable results for our lives and business activities. But how do we know we can rely on them? How do we know they are not doing anything devious or unreliable in addition? I'm not talking about a science fiction based world where they are deviously trying to replace mankind – but more about the day to day processing of transactions.

There are two main ways that programs are changed:

1. By projects to replace or make major changes to software.
2. By change control processes to make more minor ongoing changes.

In this chapter we will consider the risks, controls and audit of the development of new applications and changes, in particular:

- The traditional processes, and more modern, development lifecycles – from adoption of an idea to fully functioning software.

- Change management.

For each of the above we will consider their risks and controls, and provide some case studies and some guidance on documenting and assessing controls.

Project lifecycle overview

Let's start with some definitions:

> *Project: "A task requiring considerable or concerted effort."* Collins English Dictionary

> *"At its most fundamental, project management is about people getting things done."* Dr Martin Barnes, APM President 2003-2012

There are a number of ways and tools for representing an IT project. A typical project lifecycle for a system development project could be summarised as follows:

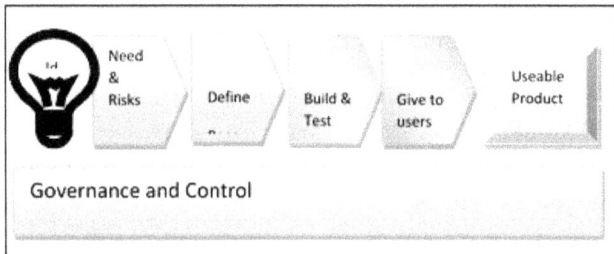

Figure 3: Summarised project lifecycle
Source: Agile Governance and Audit

Most businesses have more suggestions and ideas for changes than they can handle, with the resources they have available. They therefore need to challenge these and see which are worthwhile. Before commencing any work on a potential project, there are four basic questions that need to be considered:

1. What is this project trying to do? This should be represented clearly in some form of business case, demonstrating the benefits/changes/improvements the project delivers.

2. Who is this project doing it for? The beneficiaries should be clearly identified, ideally showing their level of commitment to the change and how they will benefit.

3. How are stakeholders engaged? The representative senior stakeholders should interact fully with the project through the whole lifecycle.

4. How does it fit in with the rest of the organisation's systems and processes? It should be making better use of existing tools wherever possible.

If the answers to these four questions are not clear – then the likelihood is that the project is doomed to failure from the outset, irrespective of the skills and disciplines of project management because (even if there is a good business case) there will not be the desire/drive in the business to change, or insurmountable technical difficulties will emerge. These four questions are only an indicator, other factors may need to be considered but they will alert the project reviewer to an increased likelihood of project risks that we will discuss later.

In the vision/needs and risks phase (aka business case), the business identifies the need for the development and expresses this in terms of business benefits. Within any organisation there may be lots of different competing ideas for development. Not all will be achievable with the resources available. The organisation therefore needs to prioritise ideas into a portfolio – ranked according to the need and business benefit. This also enables management to align the demand to their own strategic plans and to identify any common themes or potential for consolidated solutions (e.g. the implementation of a single ERP solution could combine the requirements for a new finance and a new sales system).

Having decided to proceed to the next stage, the organisation will define the requirements. This will consist of creating a design document to show the existing ('As Is') process and to agree an end design ('To Be process'). It should take account of all major stakeholders and be focused on the identified business requirement and potential benefits. The extent of the design can very – in some organisations it may be a highly detailed design document, in others it may be much simpler. Whichever approach is used at the end of the design phase, there should be a clear view as to the specific requirements.

The next phase is to build the solution. This will start with the decision of what is to be built. Based on the design and requirements, the organisation will consider different options – whether to extend systems it already has, with new modules or functionality, or to choose a new solution. The solution will be the best fit to the requirements but further modification will be required to meet the organisation's full requirements. The extent of the development work will determine the timing and manner of the final implementation. It will often involve the use of external developers. Increasingly, organisations are looking for out of the box solutions, which although they can tailor the data tables, management reports, process work-flows and the user interface for their own use, will not require any major changes to the actual program code. This makes it easier to implement new patches and releases of the underlying software, as they are provided by the supplier.

Once the development is complete the software will be tested – first to ensure that it works, and then to ensure that it meets the user requirements and can process the transaction load expected, and that it will not adversely impact any other systems in use.

Other than providing early stage support and maintenance (sometimes referred to as the warranty period), the IT portion of the project is then complete. However, for the system to be successfully deployed, the project needs to also consider the area of business readiness. This will involve developing and implementing the supporting processes, agreeing a deployment plan for all locations/divisions (training users, ensuring controls still operate, etc.) and change management (to ensure that the new processes are used in the way that they were intended).

A project can be small and of a short duration, or can be long and expensive (the smallest I have been involved with was a few hundred pounds sterling – the largest was $2bn and lasted over ten years in total). All projects require appropriate governance to ensure they achieve their business benefits (see risks below). The usual mechanisms include:

- A steering group or other regular meeting of senior stakeholders to monitor progress, identify any major risks and issues impacting the project, and ensure that the required outcomes can be achieved.

- 'Business process owner' or other representation from the business that will monitor what is being delivered, answer any queries on requirements or process design, and ultimately accept the solution on the business's behalf. If Agile is being used this will be the product owner.

- A project management function or office (PMO) – to plan the project, co-ordinate the different elements of the project and report to the stakeholder's/steering group. The PMO will also provide support to the project, for example in recruiting and on-boarding new staff, co-ordinating common activities, such as team meetings or testing, and in helping with liaison both within and outside of the project. The PMO will also be responsible for ensuring that the organisation's agreed project management approach and methodology (such as PRINCE2 or PMBOK®) is applied effectively.

- Quality or stage gate assessments – these are approval points during the project to assess progress and agree that the project can move on to the next stage or phase. The ultimate stage gate will be to place the software into the production environment so that it can be used by the business. There is usually a checklist of issues to be completed and approved during the stage gate assessment. In the case of the 'Go/No Go', approval to proceed may include provisional items which the project team have agreed to resolve in the short term.

- Data quality – reviewing the quality of data before and after it has been migrated to the new system.
- Post implementation reviews – a review to assess whether and how the project achieved its objectives.

In a traditional waterfall project approach, each of the phases illustrated in the above project lifecycle may be quite long, lasting several months and involving a number of sub-steps and approval gateways. In this approach each phase is completed before moving to the next – so for example development will not commence until <u>all</u> of the functionally has been designed. For large projects lasting many years, the requirements and business environment may change significantly and so the end product may be out of date before it has even been implemented. Costs and timelines can therefore be greater than anticipated. Also, there is a risk that the organisation may be missing business opportunities because it cannot respond to them quickly enough. To overcome this, organisations are adopting Agile project techniques, such as lean or scrum. These tend to focus on the outcomes of the project rather than the project process, and break the deliverable down into smaller iterations which are delivered at regular intervals (generally every 30 days). These approaches are typically less formal – the risks are minimised because of the small potential impact of each iteration. The same principles described above still apply, however, the documentation available for audit and review will be reduced. For further information see *Agile Governance and Audit (ITGP 2014)* by the same author.

Project lifecycle risks

When projects fail, the consequences for the business (and often personally for the project team) can be extremely significant. Just a quick Google of project failure will identify many instances of large and significant project failures – particularly in the public sector (e.g. see *www.nao.org.uk/*). There have been a number of surveys conducted to identify the reasons for project failure

The main risks associated with projects are that they fail to deliver:

1. On time
2. On budget
3. The identified required business benefits
4. Systems of sufficient quality or reliability, for example by introducing processing errors.

The main causes usually identified in the various surveys are:

- Lack of senior level leadership, sponsorship or accountability for the project. Without their drive and commitment, the project is unlikely to succeed.

- Poor clarity and consensus of vision as to what the project is trying to achieve.

- Underestimating the complexity of the project, not only from the IT perspective but also from the perspective of the impact on existing business processes. This could include cultural differences if the project is amalgamating business processes from different locations or entities.

- Scope creep – new requirements being added as the project progresses.

- Poor project management techniques, including transparency, monitoring of actual costs, progress and risks. This may include challenging the information provided. One project manager told me he regarded all green (or satisfactory) statuses as potential watermelon – they may be hard and green on the outside but are red and slushy when you cut them open! Unless there is the challenge of reporting, there is a risk that reporting will be optimistic and that there will be little, or no warning of imminent failures.

Project lifecycle controls

The aim of controls over the project lifecycle is to reduce the risks of not achieving the required business benefits, excessive costs and delays.

To reduce the likelihood and impact of the risks listed above we would expect to see:

Table 7: Project lifecycle controls

Expected controls	COBIT 5 Best Practice
The organisation should have a standard methodology for project and programme management, including governance requirements, to ensure consistency and benefit from lessons learnt on previous projects.	BAI01-BP1 Maintain a standard approach for programme and project management

Expected controls	COBIT 5 Best Practice
If there are a number of related and interdependent projects, a formal programme should be created to confirm expected benefits and ensure interdependencies are understood and not ignored by individual projects.	BAI01-BP2 Initiate a programme
There should be a plan to identify stakeholders and agree their needs and requirements from the activity. This includes agreeing their communication needs.	BAI01-BP3 Manage stakeholder management
The business case, scope and delivery of the programme should be planned and documented. This should be regularly reviewed and updated.	BAI01-BP4 Develop and maintain plan
The programme should be launched formally to increase awareness of the activity and its expected outcomes. This may include definition and planning of key stage gates.	BAI01-BP5 Launch and execute
Progress of the programme, and its constituent projects should be monitored so that any potential issues can be identified and rectified quickly before they have significant impact.	BAI01-BP6 Monitor, control and report on outcomes
Each project should be defined and scoped with formal approval by sponsors.	BAI01-BP7 Start and initiate projects within the programme

Expected controls	COBIT 5 Best Practice
Activities within a project should be planned, showing tasks, responsibilities, key delivery dates, cost and resource requirements.	BAI01-BP8 Plan projects
A quality management plan should be used to manage the quality of the deliverable and should be reviewed and updated regularly.	BAI01-BP9 Manage project and programme quality
A risk framework should be in place to record risks as they are identified and track their resolution. This should include an assessment of the likely impact and clearly defined timelines and responsibilities for resolutions.	BAI01-BP10 Manage programme and project risk
The performance of the project should be monitored and reported.	BAI01-BP11/12 Monitor and control projects/manage project resources and work packages
The expected outcomes of the project should be clearly documented and a formal close conducted to demonstrate that they have been achieved. This should also include a lessons learnt review so that any strengths can be repeated on future projects and any weaknesses avoided.	BAI01-BP13 Close project

Expected controls	COBIT 5 Best Practice
As for projects, the expected outcomes for a programme should be identified and after all projects are completed, checked before a formal close (including lessons learnt).	BAI01-BP14 Close a programme

In addition to the above, some organisations now have standards for application security to be included in the design and build of new systems (e.g. OWASP).

This will be increasingly important with current trends to make more use of standard (often Cloud-based) solutions so that what appears to be one system to the user is in fact many applications seamlessly joined together. In this type of design common application security is essential.

Project lifecycle case study examples

Travelling to nowhere

I was part of a review team looking at the implementation of a website and related online market places for a tour operator. I asked seven directors, all committed to the project, what its objective and expected outcome was. I got seven completely different answers ranging from to reduce costs, obtain new markets, keep up with competitors, etc.

Unless there is a clear understanding of the objectives and requirements for the project, how can you ever know whether or not it is successful? There was a real danger in this case that some of the directors were going to be disappointed with the outcome – even if it delivered the requirements of the others.

A tale of two projects

I was involved in a very important project for an airline, providing ongoing project assurance. I was very concerned about the lack of focus of the project team and their ability to deliver. So I asked the project sponsor (the acting CEO) to attend the meeting and set the context of the significance of the project to the business. An hour and a half into the meeting and he still had not appeared. He then stuck his head round the door and said – there's a party downstairs, why are you not all there? The meeting abruptly broke up – not the outcome I wanted.

On another project with another organisation, at the start of a two-day business awareness workshop the CEO for the whole of the US attended and clearly stated the importance of the project and why it was important to the business. This focused the workshop and ensured we had a successful outcome.

Project lifecycle documenting, assessing and testing controls

There are two main aspects to system development audit:

1. Audit of project/programme management.

2. Audit of the project/programme management of a project or programme.

There is a good deal of debate as to the best timing for a review of application development. The concern is that if the auditor becomes too involved in the project, they become part of the project and therefore lose their independence. My personal view is that it depends on the level of the risk for a project. A high-risk project should have regular assurance reviews, either from internal audit or from some other independent assurer. The review should include all of the controls listed above – based on:

1. enquiry of project management, team members and stakeholder representatives.
2. obtaining evidence to confirm controls are operating effectively, particularly:
   o Documentation and monitoring of project/ programme
   o Risk assessment and resolution
   o Programme/project governance frameworks.

It is important for the auditor to maintain a healthy professional scepticism when gathering evidence. Consider the following two examples:

1. Control is that there are weekly project meetings involving all workstream leads, chaired by the PMO, and actions recorded. *This looks good and at first look the 20-page progress pack with ten general slides, six workstream pages and list of actions is great.* But when you look at a series of these you can start to see issues that have no progress that may indicate the

project is not dealing with the critical design problem or interface that will cause it to fail.

2. Control is that the PMO monitors weekly test results and assesses progress to completion. *It doesn't take long for an auditor to check the rate of testing, the rate of defect resolution and come up with a reality check on whether testing is going complete on time. So often this exposes the magical 'hockey stick' where somehow all the open tests and defects will resolve themselves in the last week!*

Change management overview and risks

Within IT infrastructure and applications there will be frequent requests to make modifications and changes. The ITSMF (ITIL) definition of the mission of change management is:

> "To manage all changes that could impact on IT's ability to deliver services through a formal, centralised process of approval, scheduling and control to ensure that the IT infrastructure stays aligned to business requirements."

I would make two minor changes to this – firstly to add 'or software' after IT infrastructure and secondly to add 'and operates effectively and efficiently' at the end of the last sentence.

The main risk is that if unauthorised or untested changes, both scheduled and emergency, are made to the production environment, the change may:

- make the system/IT infrastructure unstable, or allow unauthorised access.

- damage controls or other integrity of the application/IT infrastructure.

- not work effectively in correcting the problem.

- cause version control issues. For example, if two people try to change the same software programme at the same time, there is a risk that the changes made by one may overwrite the changes made by the other.

- not be an effective use of resources, as a cheaper and simpler way of making the same change may have been available.

Change management controls

We would expect to see the following controls

Table 8: Change management controls

Control	COBIT 5 Best Practice ref
Authorisation included in the process to evaluate, prioritise and agree change requests.	BAI06-BP1 Evaluate, prioritise and authorise change requests
Arrangements in place for emergency changes including, restrictions on definition of what can be classed as an emergency change access control to production system, review and post-approval of change.	BAI06-BP2 manage emergency changes

Control	COBIT 5 Best Practice ref
Changes are tracked to ensure they are completed and tested. Also, reasons for rejection of a change are logged for reference if same change is re-submitted. This also enables root cause analysis to identify reasons behind common issues.	BAI06-BP3 Track and report change status
Formal closure of change requests when completed to confirm have met user requirement.	BAI06-BP4 Close and document changes

Change management case study examples

Bigger debt than expected

A senior member of IT staff left an organisation owing money for a car loan. The organisation agreed that he could work on Saturdays to work off the loan – even though he had left. The changes he made were conflicting with those made by other consultants on the new hardware during the week and so were causing additional re-work. It was cheaper and simpler to write-off his debt.

All change (NOT)

An organisation made non-standard changes to the core software of its ERP system. This meant that not only could it not take standard updates provided by the supplier but also it could not update the underlying operating system. This increased the risk of unauthorised access as security patches could not be applied, also other application systems became unstable as they were having to use old versions of the operating system.

Documenting, assessing and testing controls

An audit of change management is likely to include:

- Review of the agreed process and supporting documentation
- Enquiry and confirmation that the change process is applied effectively and consistently – including identifying any known exceptions, such as emergency changes
- Obtaining a log of changes and review for approval
- Review of sample of changes to ensure documented, approved and tested prior to promotion to production environment.

Summary

Change, including the implementation of new systems and processes, is inevitable. In order to reduce the risk of losing integrity of IT infrastructure and systems there is a need to ensure that appropriate controls are built in.

CHAPTER 8: SERVICE MANAGEMENT AND DISASTER PLANNING

Introduction

Data and information are vital to the management and operation of modern organisations. To communicate, make market offerings and sales, receive income, obtain goods and services, pay staff, and report to stakeholders, regulators and shareholders, requires access to data and computer processing capability. Just consider the frustration when your PC does not work correctly in the office. The availability of IT services is now vital to the normal operation of all organisations. In order to maintain 24 hours a day, 365 day a year (24 x 365) operations, organisations need to ensure that they have arrangements for:

- Monitoring their service availability and for reporting and escalating any incidents that occur (service management).

- Dealing with any critical loss of IT or other business resources, as a result of a natural or man-made disaster incident, so that they can continue business operations.

In this chapter we will consider both the service management and business continuity aspects of availability of services and how they should be audited.

Service management overview

The area of service management has seen significant changes during my career. As part of my training in 1981 I spent three months on secondment to the IT department of a large local authority. Most of the computing was on a central IBM mainframe – the finance department had the only PC – a Commodore Pet, and this was kept in a locked room, access for which was only granted when you signed a log for the key. The mainframe itself was kept in a secure, highly controlled environment. All operations were centralised in IT so if the service was not available it was known to the IT department and they would fix accordingly. IT processes were scheduled at specific times (e.g. payroll run on Thursday mornings). Access to the mainframe was 8 am to 6 pm, Monday to Friday. Data input was performed by a central team based upon (paper) forms completed by the end user.

Nowadays:

- Much of the data input, and some routine management, such as performing batch runs or running reports, is now performed by end users using automated processes. This includes the performance of some basic control processes (e.g. running additional backups).

- PCs and other mobile devices are everywhere in organisations. They are vital to accessing information and resources people need to do their jobs.

- Access is required around the clock, every day, in all sort of locations, not only in organisations and offices but also in coffee bars, on transport, in hotels, etc.

- The loss of even an hour of access to IT resources can have a significant impact on user's efficiency and effectiveness.

- Mainframes have effectively disappeared – to be replaced by servers and even 'the Cloud'.

8: Service Management and Disaster Planning

The basic principles of service management still remain the same, organisations need:

- Mechanisms to deliver IT services and resources including:
  - o Agreed levels of deliverable service management (e.g. the ability to provide new users with laptop devices and system access within, say, 24 hours)
  - o Ability to identify when resources are reaching capacity (e.g. email mailboxes or file storage are reaching limits)
  - o Availability management
  - o Service continuity management
  - o Ability to operate within the budget and resources available.
- Arrangements to support the provision of IT services, including:
  - o Reporting, logging, investigating and resolving incidents
  - o Managing problems to ensure they are resolved effectively and in the right timeframe and that root causes are identified, to prevent recurrence of the same issue in the future
  - o Providing service desk support to minimise any disruption caused by faulty equipment or software
  - o Managing the release of new operating and application systems into the production environment
  - o Managing the configuration of the network and other IT assets and software
  - o Management of changes made to the network and operating environment.

Risks

The main risks associated with service management are the loss of availability of IT resources required for business operations – leading to lost income and increased costs. In some industries there may also be regulatory or public image consequences of such losses.

Table 9: Service management risks

Risk	COBIT 5 Process ID	COBIT 5 Process
IT services may not be delivered as required/planned. This could lead to inappropriate use of limited IT resources.	DSS01	Manage Operations
Failure to promptly and fully resolve requests for resources or to resolve incidents, including security events, could result in loss of user productivity causing an impact on business operations.	DSS02	Manage Service Requests and Incidents
Failure to prevent or resolve issues or problems	DSS03	Manage Problems
Failure to prevent or resolve problems could disrupt and restrict access to resources and data causing customer and user inconvenience and dissatisfaction.	DSS04	Manage Continuity

Controls

Organisations need to have policies, service level agreements, and procedures and guidelines for their process for service management. Many of the organisations I have been involved with use the ITIL framework as a basis for their own framework. ITIL (Information Technology Information Library) is currently provided by AXELOS – a collaboration between UK Government and a large IT service provider. The ITIL best practices are currently detailed within five core publications:

1. ITIL Service Strategy
2. ITIL Service Design
3. ITIL Service Transition
4. ITIL Service Operation
5. ITIL Continual Service Improvement.

ITIL also provide certification, training, tools and the exchange of ideas. It covers all of the issues and risks identified above.

Synthetic monitoring/testing

Websites, both internal and external, are used for many mission critical aspects of business, including obtaining and recording sales, and providing access to online services. Organisations need to know that these services are operating effectively all of the time and to be immediately aware if the service is not accessible. There are a number of tools and services available to provide active monitoring (aka synthetic monitoring) of URL web addresses to ensure this, and often to run standard transactions on screens within the site. Pre-prepared scripts are used to ping the web address at specified regular intervals and confirm that they can be accessed and to monitor response times. This enables the web master or manager to monitor performance and respond to any downtime – wither via a dashboard screen, or reports, or SMS messages.

Documenting, assessing and testing availability controls

To review service management, I would consider the following:

Table 10: Service management checklists

Area	Questions and tests
Review of policies, procedures and guidelines	Are they comprehensive? Up to date? Applied in practice? How are they updated and disseminated?
Service management process	Review documents of process and also obtain evidence as to whether this is applied in practice. Ascertain whether there are any exceptions.
Service levels	Review service management monitoring reports and information. In particular, look for evidence of review by management and action being taken to resolve any issues. Include any synthetic, capacity management or similar automated testing.

Disaster planning

Introduction

A good many years ago I made a recommendation on an audit report that a medium sized local authority, highly dependent on its IT, should have a business continuity plan. They asked me how much they should spend on it – and I answered that like all insurance arrangements it was their call. I said that if they had a disaster they would wish they had spent more and that if they didn't have a disaster they would wish they had spent less. They introduced a plan – a few months later they had a fire in the computer room (nothing to do with me honest!) – as a result they had to implement their plan. At that stage they wished they had invested more resources into the plan – it was effective but had some gaps which proved expensive to resolve at the same time as dealing with the incident.

Following the Y2K scare and 911, most organisations now take business continuity and disaster recovery planning more seriously. They know that they need to have resilience to be able to deal with a range of occurrences – from the loss of a single PC or website, right up to the loss of a whole location or network. There are numerous examples to show the benefit of preparation, planning, testing and training in resolving these issues and being able to continue to do business They also know that it's not just about IT – you can have the best arrangements in the world with state of the art recovery centres and the latest equipment – but if you do not have the communications infrastructure, people and processes to go with it, you will still be unable to continue to do business with your customers. Increasingly, in the information age, it is also necessary to deal effectively with the media and be able to communicate clearly with the public, and sometimes with the family or friends of any casualties caused by the incident.

Although organisations are much more prepared now than they used to be, the problem has become more complex:

- The level of connectivity that users require is much higher. For example, the loss of Internet, email and mobile apps can critically impact business effectiveness very quickly.

- The number of different applications and services that are used to achieve just one thing (such as a mobile CRM app) is high, so there are many more points of failure (rather than just a fire in the data centre).

- More IT is now developed and/or contracted outside the IT organisation and so may not be included in the plans, sometimes with a number of different providers that may need to be involved if there is an incident.

Effective business continuity ensures that organisations are ready. To quote ISO22301:2012: "Business Continuity is the capability of the organisation to continue delivery of products or services at acceptable predefined levels following a disruptive incident".

ISO22301:2012 specifies requirements to plan, establish, implement, operate, monitor, review, maintain and continually improve a documented management system to protect against, reduce the likelihood of occurrence, prepare for, respond to, and recover from disruptive incidents when they arise. ISO22301:2012 is applicable to all organisations; however, how it is applied can be flexed, depending on your operating environment and complexity.

Risks

For a number of years there have been two statistics quoted:

- 80% of businesses suffering a major disaster go out of business in three years.
- 40% of businesses that suffer critical IT failure go out of business within a year.

Like a number of other researchers, I have been unable to trace the source of these quotes – they may just be myths. However, the fact remains that most businesses will do what they can to prevent a disaster occurring. If it does occur, they will recover faster if they have a plan that is effective and tested. Even if the business continues, the incident will impact normal business operations. So the main risks could be summarised as:

Business failure or major disruption as a result of:

- Not having an effective plan, supported by appropriate arrangements.
- The plan being out of date, for example, not taking account of new business operations or forms of IT provision.
- The plan not having been thoroughly tested to ensure that it is effective and understood by all staff impacted.

Controls

The only real control is to have a clear plan which meets the incidents you are likely to face, has been designed in accordance with your business needs and requirements, and is effectively implemented and tested. The Business

Continuity Institute (BCI) refers to this as embedding business continuity (see *www.thebci.org/*):

Case study examples

My favourite case study is one in which I had no involvement – other than as a Hampshire rate payer, when the County Council were successfully prosecuted for decisions/actions taken by the local fire service!

In March 1990 the fairly new headquarters of Digital Computing in Basingstoke suffered a fire which destroyed the building and millions of pounds worth of computer equipment. As would be expected for a major computing company, there was a good disaster recovery plan including backed up data, alternate sites, etc. and business operations were quickly resumed. However, even in this case there were lessons to be learnt. Most disaster recovery plans assumed at that time that incidents occurred whilst the building was empty – for example in the middle of the night. In this case it was during normal office hours – with over 300 staff inside the building. I believe that no-one was seriously injured.

I remember seeing a video of the incident developing (clips are still available online) and hearing a talk from the disaster recovery manager after the event. The film starts with people in the car park – looking at the office – just a normal fire alarm drill. Then someone spots the fire in the top corner of the building – it quickly spreads and people are moved to a safer distance. Then they realise their jackets and handbags, car and house keys are inside. Worse still, the falling building and fire destroyed dozens of their cars. The plan was extensive and well tested – as a result the disaster recovery team were able to adapt to the unexpected elements of the incident – mainly to assist staff (locksmiths were hired to help them get into their homes, arrangements for car hire, etc.). This was only possible because of good preparation.

Documenting, assessing and testing availability controls

An audit or assurance review should include the risks detailed in Table 11.

Table 11: Availability risks

Risk	COBIT 5 Practice ID	COBIT 5 Practice Name
The plan may not be comprehensive and may miss: outsourced or off-shored services; legal obligations; key stakeholders; critical systems, processes or staff; minimum service levels to be achieved	DSS04.01	Define the business continuity policy, objectives and scope.

Risk	COBIT 5 Practice ID	COBIT 5 Practice Name
The strategy behind the plan may not consider: all potential scenarios; the full potential impact of a disruption; expected recovery times; different recovery options; the RACI to be followed	DSS04.02	Maintain a continuity strategy.
The proposed response may not be fully defined including : skills/roles and responsibilities, critical business processes/procedures to be followed; contact details for suppliers and partners; resumption arrangements backup requirements; distribution of plans and supporting documents	DSS04.03	Develop and implement a business continuity response.
The validation plan needs to include; objectives for exercising and testing the business, realistic stakeholder exercises, roles and responsibilities schedules, post exercise debrief, arrangements for updating plan after validation	DSS04.04	Exercise, test and review the BCP.

Risk	COBIT 5 Practice ID	COBIT 5 Practice Name
Regular review of plan revisions to BIA communication and approval of proposed changes	DSS04.05	Review, maintain and improve the continuity plan.
Training and awareness	DSS04.06	Conduct continuity plan training.
Management of backup arrangements (including third parties); • Frequency (monthly, weekly, daily, etc.) • Mode of backup (e.g. disk mirroring for real-time backups vs. DVD-ROM for long-term retention) • Type of backup (e.g. full vs. incremental) • Type of media • Automated online backups • Data types (e.g. voice, optical) • Creation of logs • Critical end-user computing data (e.g. spreadsheets) • Physical and logical location of data sources • Security and access rights	DSS04.07	Manage backup arrangements.

Risk	COBIT 5 Practice ID	COBIT 5 Practice Name
• Encryption • On and off-site storage		
Assess adherence and effectiveness and approval of changes/change management	DSS04.08	Conduct post-resumption review.

Summary

To ensure availability of IT resources and data requires good service management to reduce the risk. However, contingency arrangements are still required in case these prove not to be adequate.

PART III: INTRODUCTION TO APPLICATION CONTROLS

CHAPTER 9: OVERVIEW OF APPLICATION CONTROLS (INTEGRITY)

Introduction

In addition to reviewing general arrangements for IT, the IRM manager/auditor may be asked to look at the controls within a specific application system (e.g. payroll, sales, ERP). Consider a nice, simple system. We own a shop and want to know how much stock it contains so we request a stock take. How do we know that the stock level shown on the stock take is correct? It will be correct if:

- actual stock has been independently verified/counted.
- we include every line and item of stock.
- the prices shown for each line are accurate and realistic.
- the calculation of total values is correct.
- we only include those items we own (for example, not including items we had sold already).
- we are happy that all of the stock is legal.

Now consider if we owned 2,000 hypermarkets across the country and still wanted to know the stock levels – we are likely to use a computer system – but the same principles apply. We would expect the controls to be embedded within the computer system rather than relying on manual controls. But we still need the same assurance over:

- Completeness
- Accuracy

- Existence/authorisation/ownership
- Presentation/disclosure.

These are very important for accurate financial reporting and are used in SOX and external auditing (often referred to as financial statement assertions). The same principles can, however, be applied to any computer system.

In this chapter we will explore application risks and the application controls we would expect to be built into systems to mitigate them, and how they can be tested.

Risks

Just because a system has not shown signs of error does not mean that it is fully reliable, neither does the idea that the system may have been thoroughly tested in the past, or a vague idea that manual controls may compensate. Problems may be hidden for years and not observed – for example I have helped to implement new systems and when we have migrated data from the previous system we have encountered inaccuracies – at first people blame the new system but it often becomes apparent that the data errors have existed in the data for some time and were not identified by the previous system.

The risks can be summarised as follows:

- Errors are introduced which cause mis-financial or other reporting.
- Failure to complete business transactions, causing additional cost and loss of income.

- Customers are not treated fairly because of system errors or failures, leading to loss of reputation and in some cases regulatory or legal fines.

- Additional work and cost required to correct errors.

These errors or incidents will be down to:

- Incomplete processing – either missing records or missing vital information from within the record (e.g. customer address).

- Inaccurate data – this could be due to input errors (e.g. date formats incorrect), or due to calculation or other processing errors (e.g. calculation of a customer's balance, expiring date of a contract).

- Transactions being performed by unauthorised, or untrained users.

To be able to rely on the performance of application controls we need to ensure that the general IT controls are adequate. This link between the two is often ignored. But if we are relying on a control built into the system it could become ineffective if unauthorised or untested changes were made to the program code. Application controls will also be less effective if there are super-users with access rights that enable them to avoid the normal control processes (e.g. for the bulk upload of data).

Table 12: Bug stories

Some (in)famous bugs
'First actual case of a bug being found' – was actually a moth found in computer relays at Harvard University in 1947.
In 2005 a famous store in the UK offered widescreen TVs for 49 pence, instead of over £350. They sold 10,000 before anyone noticed the mistake.
Y2K In the early days of computing, space to store data was at a premium. To save storage space, dates were often abbreviated so '1960' would be stored as '60'. This was OK until the year 2000 when the calendar clicked over – so how would we know whether '01' was meant to be 1901 or 2001? This caused a massive scare, with many organisations having to re-write, or in many cases, replace old software. As it turned out, the impact of the bug was very minimal. Watch out for the 2038 bug!

Controls

There are two main types of application controls:

1. Preventative – stop errors or other irregularities being introduced.
2. Detective – discover and report errors or other irregularities after they have been introduced.

Most systems will include a mix of the two – especially for high risk areas, such as controlling access (see below). Preventative controls are generally more efficient and effective as they reduce the amount of work to correct data. Detective controls are preferred by some auditors (who like something they can 'tick') and can also be useful as an indication of the integrity of the system. For example, following a system change a detective exception report may indicate a large number of error conditions if the change has impacted a preventative control – say, for example, a control to ensure the format of a date is in a certain range. Detective controls are also useful to ensure that the preventative controls have not been circumvented. For example, data may have been entered by a different route.

Preventative controls are often seen as being 'better' than detective controls because they stop things from going wrong. However, other controls that rely on manual review, authorisation, or approval, may also stop a process and can make that process efficient. The advent of 'big data' – making powerful analytics possible, may tip the balance more in favour of detective controls, reducing the level of approval but using real-time analytics to flag up potential mistakes for manual review. The auditor will always need to apply judgment to consider:

- What is this control trying to do?
- Is it designed to achieve it?
- What impact will this have on the efficiency and effectiveness of the business process?
- What is the alternative?

Preventative controls

Most modern packages, including the large ERP systems, contain preventative control facilities – these do, however, need to be configured and activated. These include:

- Data input controls – for each field input can check and either warn the user, or prevent further processing until the error has been corrected:
  - o Ensuring data input is authorised
  - o Ensuring data is entered for key information (mandatory fields)
  - o Format of data (e.g. dates, numbers, alphanumeric)
  - o Range the data lies in/reasonableness of data/sequence checking
  - o Prevention of duplicate data entry
  - o Relationship to other records
  - o Attempt to delete a record or field.
- Processing controls:
  - o Controls similar to data input controls (see above)
  - o Cross checking of data between different tables
  - o Routing transactions via a pre-defined workflow for authorisation.
- Access controls to identify and assess users before they are given access to systems and resources.

These controls can be applied to all data – both 'master data' (such as customer address details, record types, etc.) and transactional data (e.g. orders being placed).

Detective controls

Detective controls usually involve some form of reporting – either by creating a paper or soft report (e.g. in MS Excel format) or by sending an email or SMS alert. Examples include:

- Exception reports or dashboards – to show when an error has been created so that it can be corrected. Reports or dashboards to confirm that processes have completed satisfactorily (e.g. by providing totals and balances).

- Reports for reconciliation and other manual controls (e.g. stock checks).

- Audit trails –to show details of changes made to records, batch processing runs, etc.

- Embedded audit modules/automated testing (e.g. synthetic tests).

Controls over user access

Access to data and system functionality should be restricted, based on the level of least access, depending on the user's legitimate needs to access the system. Access can be restricted:

- to functions, menus, screens, or even individual fields.

- geographically or by other structural distinctions (e.g. by operating branch).

- to ensure users do not exceed their delegated authorities to perform transactions (e.g. that they can only make refunds up to a certain value).

- to ensure segregation of duties so that users cannot both create and authorise the same transaction.

Delegation of authorities ensures that people can only perform transactions up to their designated limits. For example, you go into a car showroom and want to purchase a car. When you ask for a bigger discount, the salesperson may need to get it authorised by the sales manager first.

Segregation of duties and delegation of authorities are areas of great interest to auditors, especially in organisations impacted by Sarbanes-Oxley or other compliance frameworks. One way to do this is for people to do more, rather than having to refer the issue to someone else for completion. Segregation of duties reduces the risk of error or fraud by ensuring that, for example, the person creating a transaction cannot also authorise it. Another example may be that you make a purchase in a shop and the cashier mistakenly enters £500 rather than £5. To correct the transaction, a supervisor may be required to use a special transaction. In this case the transactions of cash sales and refunds have been segregated. In some cases, management may wish to accept the risk, or there could be other compensating controls (in the example given the supervisor could review a report of refunds made at the end of each day).

Case study examples

An analogy for segregation of duties:

Farmer Georgina has a problem. She has come to a river and only has a small boat – she can only carry one item at a time. With her she has corn, a fox and chicken. The fox and chicken cannot be left alone, nor can the chicken and the corn. Georgina needs to cross the river with all three. How can she organise this?

One way to represent the problem would be a table that shows what can and what cannot be left together on one bank of the river and this could be used as a basis to solve the problem:

Chicken	Chicken			
Fox	No	Fox		
Corn	No	Yes	Corn	
Farmer	Yes	Yes	Yes	Farmer

Figure 4: Summary of chicken/fox/corn problem

The same technique can be used to compare the actions of roles, transactions, or business activities and can be used for large numbers of variants.

Place order with supplier	Place order with supplier		
Register invoice for payment	Yes	Register invoice for payment	
Authorise payment	No	No	Authorise payment
Reconcile bank statement	No	No	No	Reconcile bank statement

Figure 5: Segregation of duties chart

Now consider Georgina's problem again. The main issue is the chicken, as it cannot be left with either the fox or the corn. If we were to put the chicken in a fox proof cage, away from the corn, we would no longer have a problem – we have mitigated the risk. The problem can be once again solved – and it will take fewer trips for Georgina to get all three across the river.

We have created a mitigating control – we could do the same for the purchasing example by building a workflow to prevent the user authorising transactions they have created – they would then be able to both create transactions and authorise those created by other users.

Documenting, assessing and testing application controls

A review of application controls will consider:

- What are the specific risks for this application and its main data, in terms of financial assertions, regulatory and compliance risk?

- Documentation of preventative and detective controls in system documentation and process flows.

- An assessment of whether these controls would mitigate the risks identified if they operate as designed ('design effectiveness').

- Evidence of testing performed to confirm the controls operate as designed.

- Re-performance of testing – to confirm that controls operate in the production environment. This is often referred to as test of operating or implementation effectiveness. This could be re-testing in production under very controlled circumstances, or could be other evidence, such as version control, to ensure production and test environments are consistent.

Summary

Application controls ensure that systems perform as required and give valid outputs and results. They can be more effective than manual controls – once set up the computer will always perform the control in a consistent way until the system is changed. The main risks to consider are the financial statement assertion (completeness and accuracy) and also compliance and regulatory control.

Further reading

See *www.infosecinstitute.com*.

PART IV: LIFE AS AN INFORMATION RISK MANAGEMENT SPECIALIST

CHAPTER 10: PLANNING, RUNNING AND REVIEWING INFORMATION RISK MANAGEMENT ASSIGNMENTS

Overview

There are a variety of assignments that an information risk manager/auditor may be asked to undertake using their specialist knowledge and skills. This could be:

- A regular review or audit of a particular topic to provide ongoing compliance comfort (e.g. part of internal audit plan or regular management testing for Sarbanes-Oxley compliance).

- As part of a bigger team on a large assignment (e.g. the external financial audit of an entity, due diligence review of a potential acquisition target).

- A specific review of a particular issue – (e.g. response to a denial of service attack, health check review of an ERP implementation project).

Stages of a review

I find the Kaizen cycle for continuous improvement a useful tool for considering assignments. The cycle involves four steps (PDCA – Plan, Do, Check, Act) that are repeated as part of a continuous improvement cycle. For example, the first iteration may be that an organisation does not have a disaster recovery plan. Once this is in place, future iterations may be to improve the quality of individual elements of the plan.

Plan – this involves establishing and agreeing the objectives, process and deliverables required. The extent of planning will depend on the size of the activity or project.

Do – using the agreed plan to execute the process and deliver the required product or outcome. This includes gathering information for the next stages.

Check – compare the actual to expected results, for example by testing, to ascertain any differences or deviations from the plan. For an audit report for example, 'check' could be agreeing factual accuracy with the key stakeholders.

Act – (or Adjust) – make corrections for any significant deviations identified during the check phase.

I find the cycle useful in two ways:

1. To understand the nature of the assignment and how it will help the client.

2. To look at the lifecycle of the assignment itself.

We will explore both of these concepts in the rest of this chapter.

If our work is part of a bigger assignment, the IRM specialist may be involved at any or all of the PDCA steps. However, in my experience we are often forgotten and brought in during the later stages of a review – causing time pressures for completion in line with the rest of the assignment. The best way to deal with this is to have a close working relationship with other teams and be aware of their upcoming assignments.

The objective of the review should be to provide a level of assurance that the risks are covered and/or make recommendations as to how controls can be improved.

IRM assignment planning

To quote an old saying 'failure to plan is planning to fail'. Time spent planning can avoid issues and problems later in the review. Planning can be at two levels, to cover:

1. Extent of coverage of all assignments within a programme of reviews.
2. An individual assignment.

The overall plan for all reviews may be part of an annual or strategic plan, or could relate to a particular area (e.g. over the lifecycle of a project to implement a new system). There may be tools for this plan – or it could be a spreadsheet. Some organisations are now using Scrum and Agile rather than traditional audit planning (TAP) to agree plans. In either case, planning should be based on perceived risks, including emerging risks. If Scrum is used, you may find an 'audit product backlog' rather than an audit or compliance test plan.

In planning assignments, we need to determine the following:

- Objectives for the review – what are the risks we are to assess?
- The scope (and limitations) of the review (e.g. does it cover more than one site? How does this review fit into the overall plan?).
- Resources required to complete the work.

- Timeline and reporting requirements.

- Findings of previous, similar or related reviews (for follow-up) – also, any other reviews that are planned for the same area (e.g. from external audit).

- Relevant organisation policies, standards and guidance.

- Best practice policies, standards and guidance (e.g. ISO27001, COBIT 5).

- Key stakeholders and other actors.

The most important item is to clearly understand the scope and objectives for the review. It is useful here to use the CIA mnemonic (Confidentiality/Integrity/Availability) to assist thinking – see example below.

Example of assessing risks

Scenario: A garden centre is considering implementing online sales of its goods and services. You need to plan a review of the arrangements.

Confidentiality

Will need to ensure appropriate levels of security over:

- Customer data will need to be secured – particularly master data of customer details and transactional data, such as credit card details.

- Standing information price lists, deals, discounts, etc. will need to be secured.

- Verification of customers will need to be identified on the system. Will they have user IDs, passwords, etc.? What if they forget them?

Integrity

Need to ensure that:

- prices are correctly calculated.
- stock availability is accurate.
- deliveries are made as promised.

Availability

Need to ensure that the system is available when required by customers and outages are identified and resolved. Also ensure that adequate disaster recovery arrangements are in place to reduce impact on customers.

The plan should be documented and agreed by the key stakeholders.

Conducting an IRM review

The nature of the fieldwork will depend upon the assignment. In summary, it is likely to consist of:

- Preparing a work plan
- Review of available documentation
- Enquiry
- Verification/testing to confirm answers from enquiries
- Assessing the information obtained to reach a conclusion on the objective and identifying any recommendations.

The work plan breaks the assignment down into individual aspects and identifies the objective for that part of the review and how it is to be completed – for example, the specific documents to be reviewed, staff to be interviewed, etc.

When reviewing documentation, making enquiries or testing, it is important to keep good working papers. These should show the objectives, findings and conclusions/recommendations. Working papers should be sufficient to support the findings and conclusions, and to allow a competent person to repeat the work and arrive at the same conclusion. They also enable similar audits to be undertaken in the future. I have had some bad experiences as an auditee where I have been repeatedly asked the same questions by different teams of auditors or assurance specialists.

Reviewing the audit review

Once work has been completed, it needs to be checked for factual accuracy and quality. Confirming factual accuracy with those being reviewed ensures that there are fewer embarrassments later in the process – a review can lose credibility if findings and recommendations have to be changed or removed. The discussion of findings also reduces the risk of nasty surprises for those being reviewed and gives them time to consider how to respond. I remember on one occasion discussing a finding about lack of handover arrangements between shifts of operators – they agreed and a new procedure was in place in time for the next shift change!

The quality review is to ensure that the objectives for the review have been met and that the working papers and report are aligned with the findings. Having worked in the Big4, this form of review is normal for me – but for some it can be daunting. Such reviews are necessary to ensure consistency of work and reporting. My most common review point to raise is 'So what?'. I have found that technical specialists, for example, can raise an issue without fully explaining the implications or impact. For example:

> "Password policy to specify length and format of passwords is not complied with for the new system."

Whilst this may be accurate and concise it does not convey the impact to a lay reader. It is far better to state something like

> "There is an increased risk of unauthorised access, leading to loss or fraud, because the password policy to prevent easily guessable passwords has not been complied with."

The final check will be the issuing of the report and agreeing actions to be taken.

Ensuring action after the review

Having completed the review and issued the report, management should prepare an action plan to implement any findings, depending on their priority and urgency. They should also ensure that the findings are shared with any related areas. As an auditor I have often prepared a number of reports (or even follow-up reviews at a later stage) where the findings are the same. Whilst using the word swap facility on MS Word, etc. is an easy way to complete reviews, it is not an effective way to improve the control environment of an organisation. There should also be a mechanism to review and report on the progress of the action plan. The use of key performance indicators is a good way to ensure actions have been implemented and continue to operate effectively. They give an early warning of any changes so that management can investigate root causes and take appropriate actions.

Summary

Planning and the process of undertaking an IRM audit or assurance exercise is no different to that for any other area. The tools used and form of analysis may be different. There is also a need to ensure that a proper logical process is used for the review, and that findings are supported by good analysis and working papers. The process is less important than the outcome which should be to provide a level of assurance that the risks are covered, or to provide recommendations as to how this can be achieved.

CHAPTER 11: PERSONAL DEVELOPMENT AND QUALIFICATIONS

Overview

I enjoy my career as an IRM consultant and auditor. It has given me so many opportunities over the last 35 years and I have developed and applied many new skills, met some (very) interesting people and have been involved in a number of high-profile assignments. I have hundreds of contacts who have had equally rewarding careers. All of us have different skill sets, sector experiences, etc. – even those I trained with. Often it is about responding to opportunities as they arise – certainly that's how I came to specialise in airlines and I've thoroughly enjoyed it.

Who are IRM auditors?

Information risk management consultants/auditors fall into two main groups – what I call the 'Techies' and the 'Accountants'. Both do similar work but come from different backgrounds.

The 'Techies' come from an IT operational or development background.

The 'Accountants' have trained in internal or external audit and may be qualified accountants. Since the mid 1990s accountancy firms have been taking graduates on as specific IRM trainees and helping them to qualify as accountants, as well as providing training and work assignments specific to IRM.

The most effective IRM professionals have a strong combination of the two skill areas. Those with a techie understanding should read more broadly on business and the accountants need to develop their IT technical skills. Both groups need to keep up to date with ongoing developments and I find the best way to do this is to talk to my clients about their plans and then research areas which are new to me online. Newsfeeds from (for example) *Computing Weekly* and professional firms can often provide a quick digest of ideas and access to papers that give a more detailed understanding.

A typical generic job description is shown in the box below:

IT Risk Manager/Auditor/Assurance Manager

Responsibilities

To provide management with feedback and comfort on the IT risks and adequacy of governance and controls. This involves:

- Coordinating, planning, scoping, budgeting and completing IT audit assignments based on areas of highest risk.

- Identifying any areas of weakness in IT infrastructure, projects and systems, that would increase the risk of loss through error or fraud.

- Developing and performing testing and obtaining evidence to support conclusions.

- Designing appropriate, practical, effective and efficient controls frameworks.

- Working with business, project and finance management, and with other risk management and audit specialists to improve the IT controls and governance framework.

- Adhering to the organisation's policies, auditing standards and professional ethics.

- Reporting audit findings and recommendations to the audit manager, with clear recommendations and conclusions.

- Maintaining comprehensive and accurate audit working papers.

Skills and attributes

- A general knowledge and awareness of current IT risks and issues (e.g. project risks, cyber security).

- Technical competence and ability to grasp complex issues quickly and effectively.

- Ability to communicate with those from both technical and non-technical backgrounds and to explain IT, governance, risk and controls concepts.

- Strong analytical and report writing skills.

- Tenacity to ensure that issues and risks are resolved.

Qualifications

- Usually educated to degree level, but may have come from a strong IT background ('Qualified by experience').

> - May have an accounting or audit qualification.
> - Possess or working towards one of the following qualifications:
>   - o ISACA (CISA, CISM, CRISC)
>   - o Certified Information Security Professional (CISSP)
>   - o Other specialist qualifications as appropriate, depending on specialism (e.g. ISO27001, APM, ITIL, PRINCE2).

Skills audit

To help develop your career it may be useful to complete a skills audit. This involves an honest personal assessment of your skill set against the common areas covered by an information risk management auditor. You can then identify which areas you want to develop. I once applied this and got a response from someone showing they were an expert in all areas. I would say this is impossible! The aim is to have a base level of knowledge and skill across the spectrum and to be able to demonstrate deeper skills in two to three areas.

I use a seven level key:

0   No knowledge

1   Basic understanding

2   Have sufficient awareness to be able to discuss the high-level concepts and principles

3   Capable of conducting a review independently

4   Have conducted and/or reviewed a number of assignments successfully

5 Capable of conducting a deeper review into specific specialist areas (e.g. ERP systems, technical security, etc.)

6 Seen as an expert both within and outside your organisation – consulted by others undertaking a review in this area

But you could develop your own scale. I have provided a template for an initial assessment below. This could be used as a basis for developing a more detailed matrix.

	Level (0-6)	Is this your desired level?
Technical		
General IS controls audit		
Information security		
System development/ project lifecycle		
Business continuity and disaster recovery		
Current trends and issues		
Application controls		
Soft skills		
Assignment planning		
Risk analysis		
Interviewing and data gathering		
Report writing		
Training and presentational		
Assignment review		

Qualifications available

The most commonly requested qualifications, and ones for which some employers will provide support, are provided by ISACA and CSSP.

The ISACA certifications available are shown in Table 13.

Table 13: ISACA certifications

Certification	Aimed at those who
Certified Information Systems Auditor (CISA)	Audit, control, monitor and assess information technology and business systems.
Certified Information Security Manager (CISM)	Are in management to design, build and manage enterprise information security programs.
Certified in the Governance of Enterprise IT (CGEIT)	Are professionals with knowledge and experience of applying enterprise IT governance principles and practices.
Certified in Risk and Information Systems Control (CRISC)	Link IT risk management to enterprise risk management to become strategic partners to the business.
Cyber security Nexus (CSX)	Can demonstrate they know the most current cyber security standards and have skills and experience showing commitment and tenacity.

All of the certifications require an examination and some include a requirement to demonstrate additional practical experience. Exams are held two to three times a year at a number of centres around the world, in different languages. Further details are available from the ISACA website (*www.isaca.org*).

A number of entrants to information risk auditing from IT wish to have a wider qualification, or may already have CISSP, provided by (ISC)²®. The CISSP exam tests the eight domains of the CISSP bank of knowledge:

1. Security and risk management
2. Asset security
3. Security engineering
4. Communications and network security
5. Identity and access management
6. Security assessment and testing
7. Security operations
8. Software development security.

Further details can be found on the (ISC)² website (*www.isc2.org*).

Professional and ethical standards

Because we are advising on best practice governance and control, we need to set good examples ourselves in the way that we undertake our work. For example, we can hardly tell users to ensure they lock their screens when not in use and then leave our own screens open when we walk away from our desks; or write down our passwords and attach them to our laptops!

Those with professional qualifications and memberships will be bound by the ethical and professional standards of their institutes. Both ISACA and the Institute of Internal Auditors, for example, have their own standards. Failure to comply could lead to the loss of a qualification standard – and in some cases the loss of your career!

The key general principles to apply are:

- Integrity – auditors must be honest and trustworthy, for example, making clear where there is a potential or perceived conflict of personal and professional interests. This includes complying with laws and regulatory requirements (e.g. not shredding vital evidence).

- Objectivity – the ability to remain balanced in undertaking assignments.

- Confidentiality – the audit will often need to have access to highly confidential information. For example, you may be asked to review systems for a proposed merger or takeover, or be involved in a confidential project, releasing knowledge of which could affect the market value of the organisation or jeopardise the success of the transaction. This needs to be safeguarded.

- Competency – maintaining professional competence, not exceeding own level of competence, applying skills and knowledge to the assignment.

- Encourage the development of sound frameworks for IT governance and control.

- Openness in disclosing all relevant information.

Some organisations require staff to complete regular business compliance and independence returns. Most institutes and societies also require members to complete some form of continuing professional development to keep their skills up to date and relevant. There could be a requirement to retain records and evidence of seminars, training, and writing of articles, professional reading, etc. This can sometimes be required for a random review.

Sources of employment

IRM managers and auditors are employed in a wide variety of roles and organisations. The main source of employment is:

- Banking and finance – due to the need for compliance and the complexity of IT operations and systems.
- Accounting firms – providing internal and external audit, and risk and compliance consultancy services.
- Public sector.
- Other large organisations – particularly in IT services and technology, telecommunications and manufacturing.

Most of the above take staff, at a variety of levels of experience, and provide training and personal development. Many IRM specialists (including myself) prefer to work as independent contractors, providing our skills on a short-term basis for individual projects or assignments.

A personal case study

My own career history may provide some ideas.

I started my working career as a trainee accountant in local government. This included time seconded to IT and internal audit. At that time there was an awareness of the need for specialists in computer audit. I was intrigued as I liked the challenge of being involved in a new area. I moved into computer audit – and was eventually recruited by KPMG as a public sector auditor. This opened up many new opportunities – and over the years I was involved in some very exciting assignments and was able to develop my skills and qualifications. I worked all over the world (Australia, Thailand, India, throughout Europe and in Canada and North America). I have chosen to specialise primarily in project risk – and over the last few years I saw a niche in auditing Agile projects so have now specialised in that.

Summary

IRM can form the basis for an excellent career. There are a number of options available and it can be both financial and intellectually rewarding.

FURTHER READING AND RESOURCES

Chapter 1

See ISO standards on risk management (_www.iso.org/iso/home/standards/iso31000.htm_)

COSO Understanding and communicating risk appetite (_www.coso.org/documents/ERM-Understanding%20%20 Communicating%20Risk%20Appetite-WEB_FINAL_r9.pdf_)

Chapter 2

See the COSO website (_www.coso.org/-erm.htm_)

Chapter 3

See _www.iia.org.uk/about-us/what-is-internal-audit/_

Chapter 5

Both ISACA and IIA provide books and other resources on cyber security: What the Board of Directors Needs to Ask

Chapter 6

Summary of world data protection legislation – see _http://dlapiperdataprotection.com/#handbook/world-map-section_

UK Cyber essentials summary – _www.gov.uk/ government/publications/cyber-essentials-scheme-overview_

Further Reading and Resources

Chapter 7

See also APM A Guide to Integrated Assurance.

Chapter 8

Lots of resources available from Business Continuity Institute – see *www.thebci.org*.

Chapter 10

Good Practice Guidance Delivering Audit Assignments: A Risk-based Approach, November 2005 (available online)

The American Institute of CPA's (AICPA) AU-C Section 300 Planning an Audit, Source: SAS No. 122; SAS No. 128

Chapter 11

ISACA website: *www.isaca.org*

$(ISC)^2$ website: *www.isc2.org*

ITGP also offers resources and training: see *www.itgovernance.co.uk*

ITG RESOURCES

IT Governance Ltd sources, creates and delivers products and services to meet the real-world, evolving IT governance needs of today's organisations, directors, managers and practitioners.

The ITG website (*www.itgovernance.co.uk*) is the international one-stop-shop for corporate and IT governance information, advice, guidance, books, tools, training and consultancy. On the website you will find the following page related to the subject matter of this book:

www.itgovernance.co.uk/erm.aspx

Publishing Services

IT Governance Publishing (ITGP) is the world's leading IT-GRC publishing imprint that is wholly owned by IT Governance Ltd.

With books and tools covering all IT governance, risk and compliance frameworks, we are the publisher of choice for authors and distributors alike, producing unique and practical publications of the highest quality, in the latest formats available, which readers will find invaluable.

www.itgovernancepublishing.co.uk is the website dedicated to ITGP. Other titles published by ITGP that may be of interest include:

- Information Security Risk Management for ISO27001/ ISO27002

  www.itgovernance.co.uk/shop/p-607.aspx

ITG Resources

- Governance of Enterprise IT based on COBIT® 5

  www.itgovernance.co.uk/shop/p-1509.aspx

- The Security Consultant's Handbook

  www.itgovernance.co.uk/shop/p-1726.aspx

We also offer a range of off-the-shelf toolkits that give comprehensive, customisable documents to help users create the specific documentation they need to properly implement a management system or standard. Written by experienced practitioners and based on the latest best practice, ITGP toolkits can save months of work for organisations working towards compliance with a given standard.

Please visit *www.itgovernance.co.uk/shop/c-129-toolkits.aspx* to see our full range of toolkits.

Books and tools published by IT Governance Publishing (ITGP) are available from all business booksellers and the following websites:

www.itgovernance.eu   *www.itgovernanceusa.com*

www.itgovernance.in   *www.itgovernancesa.co.za*

www.itgovernance.asia.

Training Services

The effective management of information risk depends on the implementation, maintenance and continual improvement of an information security management system (ISMS). The international standard ISO 27001 sets out the specifications for an ISMS, a risk-based approach to corporate information security that encompasses the whole organisation.

IT Governance's ISO 27001 Learning Pathway provides ISO 27001 information security courses from Foundation to Advanced level, with internationally recognised qualifications awarded by IBITGQ.

Our classroom and online training programmes will help you develop the skills required to deliver best practice and compliance to your organisation. They will also enhance your career by providing you with industry standard certifications and increased peer recognition. Our range of courses offer a structured learning path from Foundation to Advanced level in the key topics of information security, IT governance, business continuity and service management.

Full details of all IT Governance training courses can be found at

www.itgovernance.co.uk/training.aspx.

Professional Services and Consultancy

Managing information risks depends on determining the adequacy of your information security systems. Whether you're certified to an international standard such as ISO 27001 or follow your own processes, a good, risk-based information security posture depends on regular penetration testing to determine the vulnerabilities you present to the Internet so that you can mitigate them.

IT Governance's consultant-driven penetration tests combine a range of advanced manual tests by our expert, CREST-accredited penetration testers with a number of automated vulnerability scans, using multiple tools and techniques, to enable you to protect your web applications from malicious attack.

ITG Resources

As a CREST member company, IT Governance has been verified as meeting rigorous standards of security testing. Our clients can rest assured that our technical work will be carried out by qualified and knowledgeable professionals.

For more information about penetration testing and other IT Governance technical services, please see:

www.itgovernance.co.uk/penetration-testing-packages.aspx.

Newsletter

You can stay up to date with the latest developments across the whole spectrum of IT governance subject matter, including risk management, information security, ITIL and IT service management, project governance, compliance and so much more, by subscribing to our newsletter.

Simply visit our subscription centre and select your preferences:

www.itgovernance.co.uk/newsletter.aspx.

EU for product safety is Stephen Evans, The Mill Enterprise Hub, Stagreenan, Drogheda, Co. Louth, A92 CD3D, Ireland. (servicecentre@itgovernance.eu)

www.ingramcontent.com/pod-product-compliance
Lightning Source LLC
Chambersburg PA
CBHW070403200326
41518CB00011B/2037